FEW BOOKS
CHANGE PEOPLE'S LIVES.
READ MARIE WINN'S
THE PLUG-IN DRUG.
IT MAY CHANGE YOURS.

"Parents and teachers—indeed, all who care about the survival of the human spirit—should read this thoroughly provocative book and take heed."

—Nancy Larrick, author of *A Parent's Guide to Children's Reading*

THE PLUG-IN DRUG "may provide just the kind of hell-fire we need to rouse us from our lethargy long enough to switch off the set."

—Stephanie Harrington,
The New York Times Book Review

"We are all reading Marie Winn's book on television, my friends and myself, and marveling that what ought to be obvious has waited so long to be said. And it is said here with evidence and documentation that takes us well beyond the obvious—but not a hair away from the truth."

—Eric Bentley

"A thoughtful, lucid argument to the effect that television watching itself, rather than the contents of television programs, is what damages child development and family relations. The author draws on several disciplines . . . and blends their findings with her own research in a style that is unpretentious (no jargon) and effective."

—*The New Yorker*

THE PLUG-IN DRUG

Marie Winn

BANTAM BOOKS
TORONTO · NEW YORK · LONDON

To Allan, Mike, and Steve

THE PLUG-IN DRUG
*A Bantam Book / published by arrangement with
The Viking Press*

PRINTING HISTORY
Viking Press edition published April 1977

2nd printing	.... April 1977	4th printing	.... August 1977
3rd printing	.... May 1977	5th printing	.. November 1977

Bantam edition / May 1978
2nd printing .... August 1978
3rd printing .... July 1980

ACKNOWLEDGMENTS
Field Newspaper Syndicate, Inc.: "Dennis the Menace" cartoon
used by permission of Hank Ketcham and © 1976 by Field
Newspaper Syndicate, Inc., T.M.® *Alfred A. Knopf, Inc. and
Jonathan Cape Ltd.:* from Bullet Park, by John Cheever, Copy-
right © 1967, 1968, 1969 by John Cheever, reprinted by per-
mission. *Ladies' Home Journal:* from "Television Violence—
How It Damages Your Children" by Victor Cline, © 1975
Downe Publishing, Inc., reprinted with permission of Ladies'
Home Journal. *Newsweek:* "Ousting the Stranger from the
House" by Colman McCarthy, March 25, 1974 issue, Copyright
© 1974 by Newsweek, Inc.; all rights reserved; reprinted by
permission. *Redbook and Dr. T. Berry Brazleton:* from "How
to Tame the TV Monster" by T. B. Brazleton, April 1972,
Copyright © 1972 by Redbook Publishing Co., reprinted by
permission.

Bantam Books are published by Bantam Books, Inc. Its trademark, consisting of the words "Bantam Books" and the por-
trayal of a bantam is Registered in U.S. Patent and Trademark
Office and in other countries. Marca Registrada. Bantam
Books, Inc., 666 Fifth Avenue, New York, New York 10019.

PRINTED IN THE UNITED STATES OF AMERICA

12 11 10 9 8 7 6 5 4 3

Preface

Some of the material in this book is based on my readings of scientific papers on different aspects of television, books and articles for the general public about television, writings about child development, the family, and our various modern predicaments and dilemmas. With the exception of those ideas that have become so absorbed as to be inextricable from my own thoughts, I have tried to give the source of all the written material I have used.

A greater part of this book has its source in lengthy talks I have had about television with parents, children, teachers, social workers, television executives, school principals, child psychologists and psychiatrists. All unattributed quotations in the following pages are taken from transcriptions of these personal interviews. Most of the parents and children I interviewed belong to middle-class families in two cities, Denver and New York, and in the suburbs and outlying countryside of those cities—not a completely representative sample by scientific standards, but a remarkably varied one nevertheless, including professional, agricultural, business, academic, and artistic families of varying sizes and life styles. Some of those willing to talk to me about the television experience were my own friends, some were friends of friends and even friends of friends of friends; as people heard about my interest in problems relating to television, they were often eager to volunteer their own particular stories.

Some families were reached through advertisements I placed in the newspapers. I talked to mothers and fathers at parties, during concert intermissions, at the beach, at my own children's schools, and in my neighborhood playground, where I stationed myself for a number of weeks and where, as I talked to young mothers who never refused to answer my persistent and sometimes difficult questions, I renewed my deep sympathy for parents trying to raise young children in today's society.

Why have I limited my investigations to middle-class families, it might be asked. Partly because these are the very people whose behavior, as Philip Slater writes, "has the greatest impact on society and who have the power and resources to improve it,"[1]* and partly because my informal methods of investigation lend themselves best to areas in which I have some experience myself. Therefore I have chosen to write about families which are not very different from my own. Perhaps lower-class or upper-class families are not so very different either. I rather think they are not, but cannot say so with any authority.

What I can say with some authority, as a result of years of talking and listening to others talk about television, is that parents *need* to think about television in a new way, and need to consider the role it plays in their children's lives and in their lives together as a family. Only then can they begin to consider the need to do something about it.

Special thanks for help and encouragement to Dorothy Cohen, Nina Mack, Elspeth and Nick Mac-Donald, Janet Malcolm, Peggy McIntosh, Ellen Posner, Peggy Steinfels, Arthur and Mary Ellen Wang, Joan Winn.

Acknowledgment is due to: Irene Abosch, Karen Andres, Linda Asher; Chris and Margaret Beels; Candace Berger; Mrs. Charles Bohons; Marilynn Bonato; Mr. and Mrs. Jack Carey; Danielle and Jack Carr; Ellie Caulkins; Carol Cohen; Elizabeth Rogers Cohen and Ezekiel; Reneta Cuff; Mr. and Mrs. R. S. Culver and Joe, Bobby, Tommy, and Lisa; Naomi Danzig and Alexis and Adrian; Donnamae Davidson; Mrs. Margaret Davis; Ken and Barbara Eisold and Katherine and Elizabeth; Jill Frisch and Madeleine; Mrs.

Perry Fersko; Carol Gelber and Jed and Amy; Linda
Gottlieb and Andrew and Nicholas; Sally and Wayne
Halloway; Earl and Pat Hauck; Mrs. Darrell Harri-
son; Sue Heath; Dinny Howard and Nugget and Mag-
gie; Nina Knyphausen and Anton and Julie; Arthur
and Leslie Kopit; Betty Kramer; Penny Littell and
Fanny; Clara Longstreth; Marcia Lowe; Ethan and
Zachary MacDonald; Ken and Peggy McIntosh; Ginny
Miller and Ivan; Mary Alice Murphy; Mr. and Mrs.
Ralph Pederson and Arne and Amy; Mr. and Mrs.
Paul Peterson; Florence Phillips; George Port; Mr. and
Mrs. D. K. Porter and Randy, Laurie, and Michael;
Mrs. J. Radinsky; Barbara and Jack Radosevick; Mary
Beth Reed and Tracy and Toy; Mrs. John Robert-
son; Barbara Rosen and Sarah; Louis Rosenberg; Peggy
Rosenberry and Flip; Mrs. William G. Ross; Lowell
and Margo Rubin; Barbara Haddad Ryan; Irene Sam-
ple and Kate and Edward; Brandy and Aaron Schure;
Jaclyn Shapiro; Mrs. David Sidorsky and Robert,
Gina, and Emily; Mrs. Richard Sigtoos; Mrs. G. R.
Spendlove; Mr. and Mrs. Fred Tanquary; Joan Turn-
er; Bea Wernick; Mrs. John V. Wright.

C. Christian Beels, M.D.; Stella Chess, M.D.; Peter
Crown; Jim Day; Marshall Haith; Desmond Heath,
M.D.; Julian Hochberg; Paul Kaufmann; Edward Palm-
er; Lowell Rubin, M.D.; Rebecca Shannock; Suzy
Sholz, M.D.; Diana Siskind; Joel Solomon, M.D.; Elea-
nor Townsend, M.D.; Sidney Werkman, M.D.; Joseph
Winn, M.D.

Eleanor Brussell; Jerry Cascio; Betty Lou English;
Esty Foster; Helen G. Garrison; Evelyn Halpert; Nancy
Hedland; Aloise Heubach; Margaret Katz, Margaret
Lawrence; Virginia Paulsen; Sheila Rowe; Kay Saelens;
John Seeger; Terry Spitalny.

Contents

I

THE TELEVISION EXPERIENCE

1

It's Not <u>What</u> You Watch

Concern about the effects of television on children has centered almost exclusively upon the *contents* of the programs children watch. Social scientists and researchers devise experiments Byzantine in complexity and ingenuity to determine whether watching violent programs makes children behave more aggressively, or conversely, whether watching exemplary programs encourages "prosocial" behavior in children. Studies are conducted to discover whether television commercials make children greedy and materialistic or, as some have suggested, generous and spiritual. Investigators seek to discover whether stereotypes on television affect children's ways of thinking, causing them to become prejudiced, or open-minded, or whatever.

The very nature of the television experience, as opposed to the contents of the programs, is rarely considered except by apocalyptic thinkers of the McLuhan school who focus on the global consequences of the television experience rather than its effects on individual development. Perhaps the ever-changing array of sights and sounds coming out of the machine—the wild variety of images meeting the eye and the barrage of human and inhuman sounds reaching the ear—fosters the illusion of a varied experience for the viewer. It is easy to overlook a deceptively simple fact: one is always *watching television* when one is watching television rather than having any other experience.

Whether the program being watched is "Sesame Street" or "Superman," "The Ascent of Man" or "Popeye," there is a similarity of experience about all television watching. Certain specific physiological mechanisms of the eyes, ears, and brain respond to the stimuli emanating from the television screen regardless of the cognitive content of the programs. It is a one-way transaction that requires the taking in of particular sensory material in a particular way, no matter what the material might be. There is, indeed, no other experience in a child's life that permits quite so much intake while demanding so little outflow.

Preschool children are the single largest television audience in America, spending a greater number of total hours and a greater proportion of their waking day watching television than any other age group. According to one survey made in 1970, children in the 2–5 age group spend an average of 30.4 hours each week watching television, while children in the 6–11 group spend 25.5 hours watching.[1] The weekly average for adult viewers in 1971 was 23.3 hours.[2] Another survey made in 1971 documented a weekly viewing time of 34.56 hours for preschool boys and 32.44 hours for preschool girls.[3] Still other surveys suggest figures up to 54 hours a week for preschool viewers. Even the most conservative estimates indicate that preschool children in America are spending more than a third of their waking hours watching television.

What are the effects upon the vulnerable and developing human organism of spending such a significant proportion of each day engaging in this particular experience? How does the television experience affect a child's language development, for instance? How does it influence his developing imagination, his creativity? How does the availability of television affect the ways parents bring up their children? Are new child-rearing strategies being adopted and old ones discarded because the television set is available to parents for relief? Is the child's perception of reality subtly altered by steady exposure to television unrealities? How does watching television for several hours each day affect the child's abilities to form human relationships? What happens to family life as a result of family members' involvement with television?

Though there may never be clear-cut and final answers to these questions, the very fact that they are rarely raised, that the experience *qua* experience is rarely considered, signals the distorted view American parents take of the role of television in their children's lives.

The Experts

The child-care experts and advisers American parents have come to depend on, the Dr. Spocks, the Dr. Ginotts, et al., have ignored the television experience almost completely. In spite of the fact that television viewing takes up more of the average child's waking time than any other single activity, most popular child-care manuals devote only a few paragraphs to television, and even those refer exclusively to the content of the programs children are likely to watch. Among the pages and pages on tensional outlets, fears, anxieties, refusal to eat vegetables, and other matters, parents may find only a few banal warnings to monitor their children's television programs for violence or excessive sex. The most influential of child authorities, Dr. Benjamin Spock, makes no mention in his famous guide of the role of television in the lives of preschool children and he concludes a half-page section on radio and television programs for older children by suggesting that parents not worry too much about their children's involvement with television, just so long as they get their homework done and get to bed on time. "If the rest of the family is driven mad by having to watch or listen to a child's programs and if they can afford the expense," he advises, "it's worth while to get him a set for his room."[4] That this may be a singularly ill-considered bit of advice will emerge as the television experience is examined in greater depth in these pages.*

---

*It appears that this phrase has been excised from the latest edition of *Baby and Child Care*,[5] as well as a preceding sentence, which read: "In general, if a child is taking care of his homework, staying outside with his friends in the afternoon, coming to supper, going to bed when it's time, and not being frightened, I would be inclined to let him spend as much of his evening with television or radio as he chooses." While these deletions may indicate a new awareness of television's dangers, Spock offers no new guidance about television use or control.

Parents themselves, though often deeply troubled about television and its effects upon their children, center their concern on the subject matter of the programs their children watch, rather than on the television experience itself. Their content-centered approach is epitomized by the activities of an increasingly important parent-lobbyist organization, Action for Children's Television, known as ACT. This organization, formed in 1968 by a group of Boston mothers, grew out of the common anxieties of the founding parents about television: their children were spending too many hours watching television, the mothers agreed, and the violence that seemed to dominate children's programs was appalling. Moreover, the incessant commercial interruptions were making their children crave a variety of shoddy toys and unwholesome foods.

From a small local interest group ACT has grown into an influential national organization supported by large foundations and individual subscriptions. Though the original concern of the ACT mothers did include *how much* television their children watched, the activities of ACT were soon directed primarily toward the *content* of children's programs, especially toward eliminating violence and commercialism and encouraging the production of good entertainment programming for children.

Parents and educators greeted ACT with enormous enthusiasm and gratitude. Who would suppose that in its endeavors to improve programming for children ACT might be compounding rather than alleviating the television problem that distresses American families?

The fallacy of ACT's promise is epitomized in the words of one of its founders as she describes its aims: "We came to the realization that children watch a great deal of television that is not particularly designed for them, that parents have a perfect right to ask those responsible for programs aimed at the young to meet the *specific needs of children* [my italics] for at least a couple of hours during the day or evening."[6]

But is it the specific needs of *children* that are at

stake when parents demand better programming? Surely the fact that young children watch so much television reflects the needs of *parents* to find a convenient source of amusement for their children and a moment of quiet for themselves. It seems, then, the need of parents to assuage their gnawing anxieties about the possible effects of hours of quiet, passive television watching that underlies their desire to make those hours less overtly repugnant.

The needs of young children are quite different. The developing child needs opportunities to work out his basic family relationships, thereby coming to understand himself. The television experience only reduces these opportunities.

The child needs to develop a capacity for self-direction in order to liberate himself from dependency. The television experience helps to perpetuate dependency.

The child needs to acquire fundamental skills in communication—to learn to read, write, and express himself flexibly and clearly—in order to function as a social creature. The television experience does not further his verbal development because it does not require any verbal participation on his part, merely passive intake.

The child needs to discover his own strengths and weaknesses in order to find fulfillment as an adult in both work and play. Watching television does not lead him to such discoveries; indeed it only limits his involvement in those real-life activities that might offer his abilities a genuine testing ground.

The young child's need for fantasy is gratified far better by his own make-believe activities than by the adult-made fantasies he is offered on television.

The young child's need for intellectual stimulation is met infinitely better when he can learn by manipulating, touching, *doing,* than by merely watching passively.

And finally, the television experience must be considered in relation to the child's need to develop family skills in order to become a successful parent himself some day. These skills are a product of his present participation in family life, of his everyday experiences as a family member. There is every indication that television has a destructive effect upon family life, diminishing its richness and variety.

Thus it begins to appear that ACT and the concerned parents and educators who support it so hopefully may be misguided in their beliefs and efforts. The television experience is at best irrelevant and at worst detrimental to children's needs. Efforts to make television more attractive to parents and children by improving programming can only lead to the increased reliance of parents upon television as a baby-sitter, and the increased bondage of children to their television sets.

Oddly enough the television industry, though cynical and self-serving in its exploitation of children, often demonstrates a greater understanding of the true needs of children than its most bitter critics. In defending his station's inferior children's programs, a network executive states, "If we were to do *that* [supply quality programs in the afternoon, one of the demands of ACT], a lot of people might say: 'How dare they lock the kids up for another two and a half hours? Let the kids go out and play and let them do their homework. And let them have a learning experience.' I don't think it's incumbent on *us* to provide them with a service that is specific in those terms."[7]

It is unlikely that the networks are eschewing good programming for children out of altruism, to avoid tempting kids into watching too much television; junk, after all, is generally cheaper and easier to provide than quality entertainment. Nevertheless, the industry's cool indifference to the quality of children's television fare may be more beneficial for children than the struggle of those who insist that fine children's programs be available at all times. The preponderance of offensive and banal programs may act as a natural check on television viewing since conscientious parents are more likely to limit their children's television intake if only unsavory programs are available.

Fifty-four Hours a Week

A grotesque example of the universally misplaced emphasis on content rather than on the television experience itself appeared (and drew no comment) in an article about children's television by the pseudonymous Sedulus in *The New Republic* in 1970:

> Little children of all social classes are cooped up inside all day with few playmates and little to do. Few homes, whether in slum apartments, luxury apartments or suburban subdivisions, provide youngsters' minds or bodies with the exercise they need. You see the results in your local supermarket: irritable small fry, exhausted and bored by inactivity, driving their mothers crazy. A good television program could give these children and their mothers a lot of help. God knows little kids watch television endlessly.[8]

The author does not consider the possibility that these children are so irritable, exhausted, and bored by inactivity precisely *because* of their endless television watching, nor that they are deprived of opportunities for physical or mental exercise precisely because amusing them with television is so easy for their parents, far easier than taking them to the playground, playing with them, and dealing with them personally.

Sedulus goes on to plead for better programs for children:

> The present generation of preschoolers watches an average of 54 hours of television a week. This must give them an extraordinary exposure to standard adult English and opportunities to see many things. . . . But on TV American children don't come in contact with first rate things. They need good theater, myths, music, films, rich stories and experiences that provide some standard to set against other experiences.

Fifty-four hours a week? Preschoolers are hardly awake 54 hours a week! That much television watching barely leaves them enough time to eat and go to the bathroom. And yet the writer does not take issue

with the statistic nor express an opinion that, if accurate, perhaps this is less than a propitious state of
affairs. He is only exercised by the idea that those 54
hours are being filled with poor programs. He would
like to fill those 54 hours with fine experiences that
children could compare with their own experiences.
But what experiences of their own can they have if the
majority of their waking hours are being spent watching television? He would have to fill the screen with
images of children watching television.*

Television Savants

Parents may overemphasize the importance of content
in considering the effects of television on their children
because they assume that the television experience of
children is the same as their own. But there is an essential difference between the two: the adult has a
vast backlog of real-life experiences; the child does not.
As the adult watches television, his own present and
past relationships, experiences, dreams, and fantasies
come into play, transforming the material he sees,
whatever its origins or purpose, into something reflecting his own particular inner needs. The young child's
life experiences are limited. He has barely emerged
from the preverbal fog of infancy. It is disquieting to
consider that hour after hour of television watching
constitutes a *primary* activity for him. His subsequent
real-life activities will stir memories of television experiences, not, as for the adult watcher, the other way
around. To a certain extent the child's early television
experiences will serve to dehumanize, to mechanize,
to make less *real* the realities and relationships he

*It is amazing to note how often the 54-hour-a-week statistic is accepted
as a fact in writings about children and television. The summary of the
influential Harvard Interfaculty Seminar on Children, for instance, includes it as a credible figure.[9] Another book uses the 54-hour-a-week figure
to persuade parents not to limit their children's television viewing too
drastically: "American children . . . consume heaps of TV. Why it is
estimated that the average three-to-five-year-old child watches fifty-four
hours of TV a week. That kind of exposure is bound to influence a child's
play habits. . . . A youngster unfamiliar with TV's fare could find making
friends or breaking into the neighborhood gang a strain. He could also
become the block's 'oddball.' "[10]

encounters in life. For him, real events will always carry subtle echoes of the television world.

"I didn't so much *watch* those shows when I was little; I let them wash over me," writes a twenty-year-old who calculates that she has spent 20,000 hours of her life in front of a television set. "Now I study them like a psychiatrist on his own couch, looking hungrily for some clue inside the TV set to explain the person I have become."[11]

Inevitably parents of young children turn their attention to the content of the programs their children watch because they have come to believe that television is an important source of learning. But the television-based learning of the preschool child brings to mind the *idiot savant,* a profoundly retarded person who exhibits some remarkble abilities—one who can, for instance, multiply five-digit numbers in his head or perform other prodigious mathematical feats. The television-educated child can spout words and ideas he does not comprehend and "facts" he doesn't have the experience or knowledge to judge the accuracy of. The small child mimicking television commercials or babbling complex words or sentences learned from television, the young *television savant,* has no more ability to use his television-acquired material for his own human purposes than the defective pseudo-genius has of using his amazing mathematical manipulations.

An Insidious Narcotic

Because television is so wonderfully available a child amuser and child defuser, capable of rendering a volatile three-year-old harmless at the flick of a switch, parents grow to depend upon it in the course of their daily lives. And as they continue to utilize television day after day, its importance in their children's lives increases. From a simple source of entertainment provided by parents when they need a break from child care, television gradually changes into a powerful and disruptive presence in family life. But despite their increasing resentment of television's intrusions into their family life, and despite their considerable guilt at not being able to control their children's viewing, parents do not take steps to extricate themselves from television's domination. They can no longer cope without it.

In 1948 Jack Gould, the first television critic of *The New York Times,* described the impact of the then new medium on American families: "Children's hours on television admittedly are an insidious narcotic for the parent. With the tots fanned out on the floor in front of the receiver, a strange if wonderful quiet seems at hand. . . ." [12]

On first glance it may appear that Gould's pen had slipped. Surely it was the strangely quiet children who were narcotized by the television set, not the parents. But indeed he had penetrated to the heart of the problem before the problem had fully materialized, before anyone dreamed that children would one day spend more of their waking hours watching television than at any other single activity. It is, in fact, the parents for whom television is an irresistible narcotic, not through their own viewing (although frequently this, too, is the case) but at a remove, through their children, fanned out in front of the receiver, strangely quiet. Surely there can be no more insidious a drug than one that you must administer to others in order to achieve an effect for yourself.

2

A Changed State of Consciousness

Television Zombies

"I think that watching television is a rather remarkable intellectual act in itself," says Dr. Edward Palmer, head of research at "Sesame Street." "All the while kids are watching they're making hypotheses, anticipating, generalizing, remembering, and actively relating what they are seeing to their own lives."[1]

Mothers' descriptions of their young children's behavior hardly bear out the notion that television viewing is a rich intellectual activity:

"Charles settles in with all his equipment in front of the television set when he comes home from nursery school—his blanket and his thumb. Then he watches in a real trance. It's almost impossible to get his attention. He'll watch like that for hours, if I let him. But even though he doesn't seem quite awake, it's not as if he were asleep because it doesn't keep him from going to sleep at bedtime, whereas if he falls asleep at all during the day, even for half an hour, he has lots of trouble going to sleep at eight o'clock. I don't know what it is. He just seems mesmerized."

"My five-year-old goes into a trance when he watches TV. He just gets locked into what is happening on the screen. He's totally, absolutely absorbed when he watches and oblivious to anything else. If I speak to him while he's watching TV, he absolutely doesn't hear me. To get his attention I have to turn the set off. Then he snaps out of it."

"Tom doesn't answer the phone when he watches TV, even though it rings loudly right next to him. He simply doesn't hear it."

Again and again parents describe, often with considerable anxiety, the trancelike nature of their children's television watching. The child's facial expression is transformed. The jaw is relaxed and hangs open slightly; the tongue rests on the front teeth (if there are any). The eyes have a glazed, vacuous look. Considering the infinite varieties of children's personalities and behavior patterns, there is something amazingly alike about the peculiar state of consciousness such numbers of them enter into when watching television. Occasionally the child comes out of the trance—when a commercial comes on, when the program ends, when he must go to the bathroom—but the obvious "snapping out" effect, as his face resumes its normal expression and his body returns to its normal state of semi-perpetual motion, only deepens the impression that the mental state of a young child watching television is trancelike. There is certainly little indication that the child is active and alert mentally.

The Shutdown Mechanism

Dr. T. Berry Brazleton, a pediatrician and writer about children, has speculated on the significance of the television trance. He describes an experiment involving newborn babies that may be relevant to the television trance.

We exposed a group of quietly resting babies to a disturbing visual stimulus—a bright operating room light—placed twenty-four inches from their heads. The light was on for three seconds, then off for one minute. The sequence was repeated twenty times. Throughout the test the babies were monitored for changes in their heartbeat, respiration and brain waves.

The first time the babies were exposed to the light stimulus they were visibly startled; however, the intensity of their reaction decreased rapidly after a few times. By the tenth time there were no changes in behavior, heartbeat or respiration. By the fifteenth stimulus, sleep patterns appeared on the electroencephalogram, although it was clear that their eyes were still taking in light. After twenty stimuli the babies awoke from their "induced" sleep to scream and thrash around.

Our experiment demonstrated that a newborn is not at the mercy of his environment. He has a marvelous mechanism, a shutdown device, for dealing with disturbing stimuli: he can tune them out and go into a sleeplike state. But if we can imagine the amount of energy a newborn baby expends in managing this kind of shutdown—energy he could put to better use—we can see how expensive this mechanism becomes.

Brazleton proceeds to link this shutdown mechanism to the television trance so common among young children:

Just like the operating room light, television creates an environment that assaults and overwhelms the child; he can respond to it only by bringing into play his shutdown mechanism, and thus becomes more passive. I have observed this in my own children and I have seen it in other people's children. As they sat in front of a television set that was blasting away, watching a film of horrors of varying kinds, the children were completely quiet , . . they were "hooked."[2]

But while the sensory assault of the television experience serves to activate an immediate passive response in many young viewers, the residual effects of such experiences during a child's early development may prove to be quite the opposite. Writing in the *American Journal of Psychiatry,* a doctor presents another possibility:

I would like to suggest that the constant shifting of visual frames in television shows is related to the hyperkinetic syndrome. . . . Apart from the vapid and violent content of the programs, there are incessant changes of camera and focus, so that the viewer's reference point shifts every few seconds. This technique literally programs a short attention span. . . . I suggest that the hyperactive child is attempting to recapture the dynamic quality of the television screen by rapidly changing his perceptual orientation. . . .[3]

Similarly another psychiatrist proposes that the frenetic, over-stimulating pace of "Sesame Street" and other programs geared to preschool children may contribute to the frantic behavior observed with greater frequency among children today. These programs are "sensory overkill" for some preschoolers, who are not developmentally equipped to handle fast-paced electronic stimulation.[4]

Concentration or Stupor?

"Sesame Street's" educational director, Gerald S. Lesser, refers to children who seem to be in a trance while viewing television as "zombie viewers," and notes that the "Sesame Street" research department finds nothing alarming about the phenomenon. In their opinion a zombie viewer might absorb just as much from watching "Sesame Street" as a child attending in a more natural, alert style. "Zombie viewing," writes Lesser in his history of "Sesame Street," "may either reflect intense concentration or stupor."[5]

Until a scientific study of the television trance and the mental activity that accompanies it provides some conclusive answers, the question of whether the television trance reflects intense concentration or stupor must be answered obliquely, by noting parents' general observations of their child's state of mind while watching television. Parents universally report that television watching induces a state of greater relaxation. Thus they frequently use television to soothe and sedate an overactive child.

A number of mothers report:

"There are times when one doesn't want one's child to be so active. Half an hour before bedtime I don't want the kids getting worked up playing. I'd much rather they watch television quietly. It doesn't much matter *what* they watch."

"The school psychologist told me not to worry about Bill's TV watching. She said that he probably *needs* two hours of a *blah* activity when he gets home, to relax."

"When Davy gets home from school the TV helps him relax. He's able to turn himself off a little bit with it, in a way."

"It calms Mary down. It's really wonderful."

"When the kids get home from school they need to decompress, and so I let them watch television then, even though the programs are lousy."

It seems unlikely that an activity requiring intense mental concentration would induce unwinding, decompression, or any other highly relaxed condition. It is more reasonable to suppose that this *"blah activity"* induces a more passive and receptive mental state than is normal in a child.

Passivity

Parents' observation of the passive nature of their children's television viewing often underlies their deepest anxieties about television's effects. The word "passivity" comes up again and again in talks with parents about their children's television experiences.

Is this anxiety a product of our society's orientation toward doing and achieving? Does the fact that parents prefer their child to read, for instance, rather than to view television merely reflect our society's predilection for verbal, linear experience, as McLuhan suggests?

In bringing up a child from birth each parent witnesses a remarkable progression from total passivity and receptivity to activity and successful manipulation. For nothing could be more totally passive than the newborn infant. A mass of undeveloped nerves and powerful instincts, the newborn starts life with a steady, unfocused taking in. Certain biological mechanisms protect the infant from too much intake: a predominance of sleep over waking protects him from sensory overload in the early days; "spitting up" or vomiting protects him from an excess of food. But the infant is unable to "act" in any purposeful way. His entire existence is bound up in receiving.

By the time a child is two or three years old he has traveled an enormous distance from this newborn stage. His muscle control is advanced: he can focus his eyes, he can do complex manipulations with his hands, he can walk, he can communicate with subtlety by means of words, he can wield an enormous influence on his parents, at whose mercy he was so completely when he was born. He is full of purpose, struggling to gratify without delay his wants and desires, eager to learn, to explore, to understand. In many ways he is almost the reverse of that purposeless, powerless creature he was at birth.

In the life of a small child the television experience is an unmistakable return to the passive mode of functioning. It is quite unlike any other form of play. And thus since parental anxiety is often a finely-tuned indicator that something is amiss in the child's life parents' wide-spread anxiety about the passivity of their children's television experience may carry survival value for the child.

The Reentry Syndrome

Time after time parents note that their children's behavior seems to deteriorate *just after* they finish watching television. Because such behavior is frequently short-lived, parents don't usually make a great deal of it, but when asked specifically about their child's post-viewing behavior, most do confirm that *some* temporary crankiness or misbehavior often occurs at those times:

"We notice that they always come away from an hour or two of television watching in a terrible state: cranky, captious, tired, ready to explode. They come away from the set and try to assuage some sort of inner dissatisfaction in some way—by drinking a lot, eating, jumping up and down aimlessly."

"TV doesn't improve their disposition. They're grouchy and irritable right after they watch."

"After watching they're cross and hopped up."

"The moment the set is turned off, there's a rapid rise in their inability to control themselves. They whine, they fuss, they absolutely regress. I'll send them to their room to settle down. And it takes them a while before they're back to normal."

"When Anthony has spent a morning watching TV

he's not to be lived with. He's nervous, rude, inattentive, bored, doesn't know what to do with himself, and is quite disagreeable. Gradually he comes back to normal."

"Immediately after watching television the kids' behavior plummets downward from the normal. There'll be wild running around and that sort of thing."

"The main thing about television is the fact that there's a lot of energy there coming out at you, and you sit there passively, and it's going into you. When you turn that set off, it has to come out again. What I notice in my children is that it comes out in a very mindless way—mindless, spasmodic energy, a brief little temper tantrum, blowing up, pushing and shoving, being dissatisfied."

The meaning of that post-television crankiness and misbehavior is significant. A young child's behavior, after all, is a parent's most valuable source of information about the child's mental state and his emotional and physical well-being. An understanding of his behavior patterns, of how his behavior reflects his inner equilibrium, is essential to successful child rearing. A three- or four-year-old rarely talks about his feelings. He is unlikely to tell his mother, "I feel happy," or "I am tired," or "I am sick," or "I feel insecure." But by observing his normal behavior, whether he is playing cheerfully, full of energy and curiosity, or whether he seems uncharacteristically withdrawn or unnaturally wild, the parent may come to understand the child's needs and be better equipped to fulfill them.

When behavior takes a mysterious turn, when a child is disagreeable for no discernible reason or reacts in an unusual and unexpected way to both pleasant and unpleasant experiences—when, in short, his behavior does not follow the usual and simple rules of cause and effect as the parent understands them—then the parent has cause for anxiety. Invariably the child's inappropriate behavior pattern proves to have survival value when it is finally understood. A child, for instance, who comes home from nursery school each day in a wretched frame of mind, fussing and demand-ing attention, may provoke his parents to investigate his well-being at school; often serious problems are un-covered in this way, even though the child may never complain about school or his teacher, and may even claim that he is having a fine time.

Even more important to the child's well-being is the watchful mother's instinctive recognition that unex-plained crankiness may be a symptom of oncoming sickness. Long before the child articulates any symp-tom of sickness or physical discomfort, the knowl-edgeable mother, inspired by his peculiar behavior, whips out the thermometer, often to discover that the child is feverish and sick. In such a case the child's crankiness is the organism's symptom that something is wrong; like all symptoms, its function is to help re-store the body to its desired state of homeostasis. The mother is led by the symptom to take steps to help restore the equilibrium that has, for some reason, been destroyed.

Another condition in a child's life regularly leads to behavior that appears to serve no rational purpose, yet proves to have survival value. That condition is sleep. A night of peaceful, pleasant sleep may be fol-lowed by a dismal irritability upon waking up, both in children and in adults. The mood does not seem to be a result of the pleasant or unpleasant aspects of the activity that preceded it. Rather, post-sleep crankiness represents a sort of reentry syndrome, as the mind moves from one state of consciousness into another. The organism seems to require a certain period of adjustment when making the transition from the state of sleep to the state of wakefulness, a period that is longer for some persons than others. Post-sleep cranki-ness offers a brief period of protection against the dan-gers inherent in normal human interactions. Leave me alone, the recent sleeper begs by means of his irritabil-ity, I'm not ready to deal with you as my usual self. I'm a different person at this moment and might func-tion in the wrong way. Wait until I'm entirely awake. Then I'll behave reliably.

Bad behavior, to be sure, is sometimes purposefully used by the child to gain some desired end, to get his way, to compel his parents to submit to his will. In the case of post-television crankiness, however, the child's behavior is likely to lead to an undesired result: the parent will eliminate the desirable experience (television watching) in order to eliminate the subsequent undesirable behavior. It is logical to assume therefore that unlike a child's whining and fussing to get his way, the post-television bad behavior is not purposeful or within the child's active control. It is provoked for some inner purpose that the child is unaware of.

Is post-television crankiness a signal to parents that the child is fatigued and needs to rest? Why, then, do parents seem to consider television viewing a restful, relaxing activity and often encourage their overtired children to settle down before the television set? What form of rest is the parent to supply, following a number of hours of television watching? If anything, the child seems in need of physical and mental activity.

It is far more likely that post-television crankiness serves a purpose similar to the unexplained behavior that appears at the onset of illness, or at the end of sleep. Perhaps it must be considered in the light of both. It may be a symptom that a parent should heed, a sign that something about the experience of television watching is harmful to the child and may have adverse developmental consequences. Or it may signal a transition from one state of consciousness to another (postsleep irritability).

That post-television crankiness represents a reentry syndrome raises a particularly disquieting question: What, then, is the child's state of consciousness while he is watching television? It is clearly not sleep. Is it something other than waking? We are all familiar with drug-induced states of consciousness. Is the television-viewing child on some kind of trip, then, from which he must reenter the real world with the help of a transitional period of bad behavior?

It is a Hobson's choice for worried parents which

of these alternative theories to accept—television viewing the sickness, or television viewing the trip, or, worst of all, television viewing the sick trip. The curious thing is that none of this has much to do with *what* children watch on television, the usual concern of parents and educators. It is the fact that they *watch* that is significant. For if television viewing can be a "trip," then perhaps, like the drug experience, it can become an addiction as well.

3

Television Addiction

Cookies or Heroin?

The word "addiction" is often used loosely and wryly in conversation. People will refer to themselves as "mystery book addicts" or "cookie addicts." E. B. White writes of his annual surge of interest in gardening: "We are hooked and are making an attempt to kick the habit." Yet nobody really believes that reading mysteries or ordering seeds by catalogue is serious enough to be compared with addictions to heroin or alcohol. The word "addiction" is here used jokingly to denote a tendency to overindulge in some pleasurable activity.

People often refer to being "hooked on TV." Does this, too, fall into the lighthearted category of cookie eating and other pleasures that people pursue with unusual intensity, or is there a kind of television viewing that falls into the more serious category of destructive addiction?

When we think about addiction to drugs or alcohol we frequently focus on negative aspects, ignoring the pleasures that accompany drinking or drug-taking. And yet the essence of any serious addiction is a pursuit of pleasure, a search for a "high" that normal life does not supply. It is only the inability to function without the addictive substance that is dismaying, the dependence of the organism upon a certain experience and an increasing inability to function normally without it. Thus a person will take two or three drinks at the end of the day not merely for the pleasure drinking provides, but also because he "doesn't feel normal" without them.

An addict does not merely pursue a pleasurable experience and need to experience it in order to function normally. He needs to *repeat* it again and again. Something about that particular experience makes life without it less than complete. Other potentially pleasurable experiences are no longer possible, for under the spell of the addictive experience, his life is peculiarly distorted. The addict craves an experience and yet he is never really satisfied. The organism may be temporarily sated, but soon it begins to crave again.

Finally a serious addiction is distinguished from a harmless pursuit of pleasure by its distinctly destructive elements. A heroin addict, for instance, leads a damaged life: his increasing need for heroin in increasing doses prevents him from working, from maintaining relationships, from developing in human ways. Similarly an alcoholic's life is narrowed and dehumanized by his dependence on alcohol.

Let us consider television viewing in the light of the conditions that define serious addictions.

Not unlike drugs or alcohol, the television experience allows the participant to blot out the real world and enter into a pleasurable and passive mental state. The worries and anxieties of reality are as effectively deferred by becoming absorbed in a television program as by going on a "trip" induced by drugs or alcohol. And just as alcoholics are only inchoately aware of their addiction, feeling that they control their drinking more than they really do ("I can cut it out any time I want—I just like to have three or four drinks before dinner"), people similarly overestimate their control over television watching. Even as they put off other activities to spend hour after hour watching television, they feel they could easily resume living in a different, less passive style. But somehow or other while the television set is present in their homes, the click doesn't sound. With television pleasures available, those other experiences seem less attractive, more difficult somehow.

A heavy viewer (a college English instructor) observes:

"I find television almost irresistible. When the set is on, I cannot ignore it. I can't turn it off. I feel sapped, will-less, enervated. As I reach out to turn off the set, the strength goes out of my arms. So I sit there for hours and hours."

The self-confessed television addict often feels he "ought" to do other things—but the fact that he doesn't read and doesn't plant his garden or sew or crochet or play games or have conversations means that those activities are no longer as desirable as television viewing. In a way a heavy viewer's life is as imbalanced by his television "habit" as a drug addict's or an alcoholic's. He is living in a holding pattern, as it were, passing up the activities that lead to growth or development or a sense of accomplishment. This is one reason people talk about their television viewing so ruefully, so apologetically. They are aware that it is an unproductive experience, that almost any other endeavor is more worthwhile by any human measure.

Finally it is the adverse effect of television viewing on the lives of so many people that defines it as a serious addiction. The television habit distorts the sense of time. It renders other experiences vague and curiously unreal while taking on a greater reality for itself. It weakens relationships by reducing and sometimes eliminating normal opportunities for talking, for communicating.

And yet television does not satisfy, else why would the viewer continue to watch hour after hour, day after day? "The measure of health," writes Lawrence Kubie, "is flexibility . . . and especially the freedom to cease when sated."[1] But the television viewer can never be sated with his television experiences—they do not provide the true nourishment that satiation requires —and thus he finds that he cannot stop watching.

A former heavy watcher (filmmaker) describes such a syndrome:

"I remember when we first got the set I'd watch for hours and hours, whenever I could, and I remember that feeling of tiredness and anxiety that always followed those orgies, a sense of time terribly wasted. It was like eating cotton candy; television promised so much richness, I couldn't wait for it, and then it just evaporated into air. I remember feeling terribly drained after watching for a long time."

Similarly a nursery schoolteacher remembers her own childhood television experience:

"I remember bingeing on television when I was a child and having that vapid feeling after watching hours of TV. I'd look forward to watching whenever I could, but it just didn't give back a real feeling of pleasure. It was like no orgasm, no catharsis, very frustrating. Television just wasn't giving me the promised satisfaction and yet I kept on watching. It filled some sort of need, or had to do with an inability to get something started."

The testimonies of ex–television addicts often have the evangelistic overtones of stories heard at Alcoholics Anonymous meetings.

A handbag repair shop owner says:

"I'd get on the subway home from work with the newspaper and immediately turn to the TV page to plan out my evening's watching. I'd come home, wash, change my clothes, and tell my wife to start the machine so it would be warmed up. (We had an old-fashioned set that took a few seconds before an image appeared.) And then we'd watch TV for the rest of the evening. We'd eat our dinner in the living room while watching, and we'd only talk every once in a while, during the ads, if at all. I'd watch anything, good, bad, or indifferent.

"All the while we were watching I'd feel terribly angry at myself for wasting all that time watching junk. I could never go to sleep until at least the eleven o'clock news, and then sometimes I'd still stay up for the late-night talk show. I had a feeling that I *had* to watch the news programs, that I *had* to know what was happening, even though most of the time nothing much was happening and I could easily find out what was by reading the paper the next morning. Usually my wife would fall asleep on the couch while I was watching. I'd get angry at her for doing that. Actually,

I was angry at myself. I had a collection of three years of back issues of different magazines that I planned to read sometime, but I never got around to reading them. I never got around to sorting or labeling my collection of slides I had made when traveling. I only had time for television. We'd take the telephone off the hook while watching so we wouldn't be interrupted! We like classical music, but we never listened to any, never!

"Then one day the set broke. I said to my wife, 'Let's not fix it. Let's just see what happens.' Well, that was the smartest thing we ever did. We haven't had a TV in the house since then.

"Now I look back and I can hardly believe we could have lived like that. I feel that my mind was completely mummified for all those years. I was glued to that machine and couldn't get loose, somehow. It really frightens me to think of it. Yes, I'm frightened of TV now. I don't think I could control it if we had a set in the house again. I think it would take over no matter what I did."

A further sign of addiction is that "an exclusive craving for something is accompanied by a loss of discrimination towards the object which satisfies the craving . . . the alcoholic is not interested in the taste of liquor that is available; likewise the compulsive eater is not particular about what he eats when there is food around," write the authors of a book about the nature of addiction.[2] And just so, for many viewers the process of *watching* television is far more important than the actual contents of the programs being watched. The knowledge that the act of watching is more important than *what* is being watched lies behind the practice of "roadblocking," invented by television advertisers and adopted by political candidates who purchase the same half-hour on all three channels in order to force-feed their message to the public. As one prominent candidate put it, "People will watch television no matter what is on, and if you allow them no other choice they will watch your show."[3]

The comparison between television addiction and

drug addictions is often made by the addict himself. A lawyer says:

"I watch TV the way an alcoholic drinks. If I come home and sit in front of the TV, I'll watch any program at all, even if there's nothing on that especially appeals to me. Then the next thing I know it's eleven o'clock and I'm watching the Johnny Carson show, and I'll realize I've spent the whole evening watching TV. What's more, I can't stand Johnny Carson! But I'll still sit there watching him. I'm addicted to TV, when it's there, and I'm not happy about the addiction. I'll sit there getting madder and madder at myself for watching, but still I'll sit there. I can't turn it off."

Nor is the television addict always blind to the dysfunctional aspects of his addiction. A housewife says:

"Sometimes a friend will come over while I'm watching TV. I'll say, 'Wait a second. Just let me finish watching this,' and then I'll feel bad about that, letting the machine take precedence over people. And I'll do that for the stupidest programs, just because I *have* to watch, somehow."

In spite of the potentially destructive nature of television addiction, it is rarely taken seriously in American society. Critics mockingly refer to television as a "cultural barbiturate" and joke about "mainlining the tube." Indeed a spectacle called a "Media Burn," which took place in San Francisco in 1975 and which involved the piling of 44 old television sets on top of each other in the parking lot of the old Cow Palace, soaking them with kerosene, and applying a torch, perfectly illustrates the feeling of good fun that surrounds the issue of television addiction. According to the programs distributed before the event, everybody was supposed to experience "a cathartic explosion" and "be free at last from the addiction to television."[4]

The issue of television addiction takes on a more serious air when the addicts are our children. A mother reports:

"My ten-year-old is as hooked on TV as an alcoholic

is hooked on drink. He tries to strike desperate bargains: 'If you let me watch just ten more minutes, I won't watch at all tomorrow,' he says. It's pathetic. It scares me."

Another mother tells about her six-year-old son:

"We were in Israel last summer where the TV stations sign off for the night at about ten. Well, my son would turn on the set and watch the Arabic stations that were still on, even though he couldn't understand a word, just because he had to watch *something*."

Other signs of serious addiction come out in parents' descriptions of their children's viewing behavior:

"We used to have very bad reception before we got on Cable TV. I'd come into the room and see my eight-year-old watching this terrible, blurry picture and I'd say, 'Heavens, how can you see? Let me try to fix it,' and he'd get frantic and scream, 'Don't touch it!' It really worried me, that he wanted to watch so badly that he was even willing to watch a completely blurred image."

Another mother tells of her eight-year-old son's behavior when deprived of television:

"There was a time when both TV sets were out for about two weeks, and Jerry reached a point where I felt that if he didn't watch something, he was really going to start climbing the walls. He was fidgety and nervous. He'd crawl all over the furniture. He just didn't know what to do with himself, and it seemed to get worse every day. I said to my husband, 'He's having withdrawal symptoms,' and I really think that's what it was. Finally I asked one of my friends if he could go and watch the Saturday cartoons at their house."

One of the most illuminating and chilling descriptions of television addiction and its similarity to alcohol addiction is found in the following excerpt from John Cheever's novel *Bullet Park*. Here the protagonist, Eliot Nailles, is revealed in a confrontation with his nine-year-old son Tony over the child's television watching. Though it is fiction, the depths of the child's involvement with the television experience and the father's desperation, partly caused by a subliminal recognition that he suffers from a similar disability, are real and recognizable to a great number of secret sharers of the problem.

Nailles walked through the dining room, crossed the dark hall to the living room where Tony was watching a show. The tube was the only light, shifting and submarine, and with the noise of the rain outside the room seemed like some cavern in the sea.

"Do you have any homework," Nailles asked.

"A little," Tony said.

"Well I think you'd better do it before you watch television," Nailles said. On the tube some cartoon figures were dancing a jig.

"I'll just watch to the end of this show," Tony said. "Then I'll do my homework."

"I think you'd better do your homework now," Nailles said.

"But Mummy said I could see this show," Tony said.

"How long has it been," said Nailles, "that you've asked permission to watch television?" He knew that in dealing with his son sarcasm would only multiply their misunderstandings but he was tired and headstrong. "You never ask permission. You come home at half past three, pull your chair up in front of the set and watch until supper. After supper you settle down in front of that damned engine and stay there until nine. If you don't do your homework how can you expect to get passing marks in school?"

"I learn a lot of things on television," Tony said shyly. "I learn about geography and animals and the stars."

"What are you learning now?" Nailles asked.

The cartoon figures were having a tug of war. A large bird cut the rope with his beak and all the figures fell down.

"This is different," Tony said. "This isn't educational. Some of it is."

"Oh leave him alone, Eliot, leave him alone," Nellie called from the kitchen. Her voice was soft and clear. Nailles wandered back into the kitchen.

"But don't you think," he asked, "that from half past three to nine with a brief interlude for supper is too much time to spend in front of a television set?"

"It is a lot of time," Nellie said, "but it's terribly important to him right now and I think he'll grow out of it."

"I know it's terribly important," Nailles said. "I realize that. When I took him Christmas shopping he wasn't interested in anything but getting back to the set. He didn't care about buying presents for you or his cousins or his aunts and uncles. All he wanted to do was to get back to the set. He was just like an addict. I mean he had withdrawal symptoms. It was just like me at cocktail hour but I'm thirty-four years old and I try to ration my liquor and my cigarettes."

"He isn't quite old enough to start rationing things," Nellie said.

"He won't go coasting, he won't play ball, he won't do his homework, he won't even take a walk because he might miss a program."

"I think he'll grow out of it," Nellie said.

"But you don't grow out of an addiction. You have to make some exertion or have someone make an exertion for you. You just don't outgrow serious addictions."

He went back across the dark hall with its shifty submarine lights and outside the noise of rain. On the tube a man with a lisp, dressed in a clown suit, was urging his friends to have Mummy buy them a steamlined, battery-operated doll carriage. He turned on a light and saw how absorbed his son was in the lisping clown.

"Now I've been talking with your mother," he said, "and we've decided that we have to do something about your television time." (The clown was replaced by the cartoon of an elephant and a tiger dancing the waltz.) "I think an hour a day is plenty and I'll leave it up to you to decide which hour you want."

Tony had been threatened before but either his mother's intervention or Nailles's forgetfulness had saved him. At the thought of how barren, painful and meaningless the hours after school would be the boy began to cry.

"Now crying isn't going to do any good," Nailles said. The elephant and the tiger were joined by some other animals in their waltz.

"Skip it," Tony said. "It isn't your business."

"You're my son," Nailles said, "and it's my business to see you do at least what's expected of you. You were tutored last summer in order to get promoted and if your marks don't improve you won't be promoted this year. Don't you think it's my business to see that you get promoted? If you had your way you wouldn't even go to school. You'd wake up in the morning, turn on the set and watch it until bedtime."

"Oh please skip it, please leave me alone," Tony said. He turned off the set, went into the hall and started to climb the stairs.

"You come back here, Sonny," Nailles shouted. "You come back here at once or I'll come and get you."

"Oh please don't roar at him," Nellie asked, coming out of the kitchen. "I'm cooking veal birds and they smell nice and I was feeling good and happy that you'd come home and now everything is beginning to seem awful."

"I was feeling good too," Nailles said, "but we have a problem here and we can't evade it just because the veal birds smell good."

He went to the foot of the stairs and shouted: "You come down here, Sonny, you come down here this instant or you won't have any television for a month. Do you hear me? You come down here at once or you won't have any television for a month."

The boy came slowly down the stairs. "Now you come here and sit down," Nailles said, "and we'll talk this over. I've said that you can have an hour each day and all you have to do is to tell me which hour you want."

"I don't know," Tony said. "I like the four-o'clock show and the six-o'clock show and the seven-o'clock show . . ."

"You mean you can't confine yourself to an hour, is that it?"

"I don't know," Tony said.

"I guess you'd better make me a drink," Nellie said. "Scotch and soda."

Nailles made a drink and returned to Tony. "Well if you can't decide," Nailles said, "I'm going to decide for you. First I'm going to make sure that you do your homework before you turn on the set."

"I don't get home until half past three," Tony said, "and sometimes the bus is late and if I do my homework I'll miss the four-o'clock show."

"That's just too bad," Nailles said, "that's just too bad."

"Oh leave him alone," Nellie said. "Please leave him alone. He's had enough for tonight."

"It isn't tonight we're talking about, it's every single night in the year including Saturdays, Sundays and holidays. Since no one around here seems able to reach any sort of agreement I'm going to make a decision myself. I'm going to throw that damned thing out the back door."

"Oh no, Daddy, no," Tony cried. "Please don't do that. Please, please, please. I'll try. I'll try to do better."

"You've been trying for months without any success," Nailles said. "You keep saying that you'll try to cut down and all you do is watch more and more. Your intentions may have been good but there haven't been any noticeable results. Out it goes."

"Oh please don't, Eliot," Nellie cried. "Please don't. He loves his television. Can't you see that he loves it?"

"I know that he loves it," Nailles said. "That's why I'm

going to throw it out the door. I love my gin and I love
my cigarettes but this is the fourteenth cigarette I've had
today and this is only my fourth drink. If I sat down to
drink at half past three and drank steadily until nine I'd
expect someone to give me some help." He unplugged
the television set with a yank and picked the box up in his
arms. The box was heavy for his strength, and an awkward size, and in order to carry it he had to arch his back
a little like a pregnant woman. With the cord trailing behind him he started for the kitchen door.

"Oh, Daddy, Daddy," Tony cried. "Don't, don't, don't,"
and he fell to his knees with his hands joined in a conven-
tional, supplicatory position that he might have learned
from watching some melodrama on the box.

"Eliot, Eliot," Nellie screamed. "Don't, don't. You'll be
sorry, Eliot. You'll be sorry."

Tony ran to his mother and she took him in her arms.
They were both crying.

"I'm not doing this because I want to," Nailles shouted.
"After all I like watching football and baseball when I'm
home and I paid for the damned thing. I'm not doing this
because I want to. I'm doing this because I have to."

"Don't look, don't look," Nellie said to Tony and she
pressed his face into her skirts.

The back door was shut and Nailles had to put the box
on the floor to open it. The rain sounded loudly in the
yard. Then, straining, he picked up the box again, kicked
open the screen door and fired the television out into the
dark. It landed on a cement paving and broke with the
rich, glassy music of an automobile collision. Nellie led
Tony up the stairs to her bedroom, where she threw herself onto the bed, sobbing. Tony joined her. Nailles closed
the kitchen door on the noise of the rain and poured another drink. Fifth, he said.[5]

II

TELEVISION AND THE CHILD

"AND NOW AN IMPORTANT MESSAGE FROM YOUR SPONSOR: *GO OUTSIDE AND PLAY!*"

4

Verbal and Nonverbal Thought

"Sesame Street" Revisited

In the past the family served as the only training ground for a child's language development. That is to say, it was understood that the more parents spoke to a child, read to him, listened to him and echoed back his sounds, the more likely he was to learn to use language well.

Today, since words and phrases similar to those parents speak to children emanate from the television set, many parents believe that a young child will profit as much from giving his attention to a television program as he might if he spent that time talking and listening to a real person in real life. Indeed, with the almost universal acceptance of "Sesame Street" as a positive education experience for preschool children, many parents have come to feel that watching "educational" television programs may be a *more* profitable mental occupation than any they themselves might provide.

And yet the educational results of "Sesame Street" have been disappointing. The expectation that a program—carefully designed by the most eminent and knowledgeable child specialists—would bridge the gap between middle-class children who have had ample verbal opportunities at home and those children deprived of such opportunities has not been realized. Poor children have *not* caught up with their more advantaged peers, nor even made significant gains of any sort, though they watch "Sesame Street" faithfully year after year. Schools have *not* had to readjust their first-grade curricula to accommodate a new breed of well-prepared, "Sesame Street"–wise children with higher levels of language maturity (the prevailing belief in the first years of the program). Although children exhibit certain small gains in number and letter recognition as a result of "Sesame Street," their language skills do not show any significant or permanent gains as they progress through school.

Why, in the light of such small returns, do parents and educators continue to believe so deeply that this particular television program has so great a value for young children? It is likely that much of the widespread belief in "Sesame Street's" educational efficacy comes from highly publicized evaluations of the program's results made by the Educational Testing Service in 1970 and 1971. These findings indicated that the young watchers of "Sesame Street" did indeed make great gains as a result of their viewing experiences.[1]

In 1975, however, as part of a larger project studying methods of evaluating and reviewing research, the Russell Sage Foundation published the results of a rigorous reevaluation of the original ETS evaluation in a book—"Sesame Street" Revisited.[2] As the authors, a team of social scientists, painstakingly retraced the steps of the ETS researchers, they discovered some important discrepancies that led them to question seriously the original, highly positive findings regarding the impact of "Sesame Street."

The authors of "Sesame Street" Revisited found that the group of children who had watched the most hours of "Sesame Street" in the ETS study and who exhibited the greatest cognitive gains did not merely watch so many hours by accident. As a specially selected experimental group they had been *encouraged to watch* in a particular way, receiving extra attention in the form of personal visits, promotional materials, and so on. Their parents, moreover, knew they were taking part in a research program and thus were more likely to involve themselves in their children's viewing. It appears, then, that these children may have shown gains not because of the material they viewed, but because of the adult intervention they were exposed to.

The authors of *"Sesame Street" Revisited* suggest that it was indeed the encouragement that accompanied the experiment rather than the actual effects of the program material that caused those gains that were so widely publicized as proof of "Sesame Street's" effectiveness. Yet another finding supports this view: among the "unencouraged" children involved in the original ETS evaluation, heavy viewers of "Sesame Street" demonstrated *fewer* gains in cognitive skills than light viewers!

The Russell Sage study found evidence as well that the gap between advantaged and disadvantaged children the program had been designed to narrow might actually have *widened* as a result of widespread "Sesame Street" viewing.

The suggestion that "Sesame Street" fails in its avowed goals of fostering children's cognitive development and of narrowing the achievement gap comes as a shock to many parents. Not surprisingly, the authors note that their findings are often met with skepticism or outright disbelief by parents of preschool children. The authors offer a number of explanations for parents' refusal to be persuaded that "Sesame Street," though a delightful entertainment for young children, does not provide them with a particularly valuable learning experience:

• Parents are so impressed at any learning children achieve at so early an age that they generalize from the learning of a few things from the program to a far greater learning gain.

• Children might have learned some of the things they seem to have learned from the program simply from environmental exploration.

• Parents are misled by the narrow gains in letter and number recognition that come from watching "Sesame Street" into assuming that the children are making gains in more general cognitive areas.

• Parents are influenced by the testimony of their friends about *their* children's gains from watching "Sesame Street."

The authors also note the favorable press that "Sesame Street" has received since its inception. "If the attitudes and beliefs of parents have indeed been influenced by this publicity," they write, "it too may have contributed towards overestimating the program's effects." It is interesting to note that while the positive findings of the ETS study received prominent attention in the popular press, the Russell Sage study, a product of an equally if not more respectable scientific organization, has been ignored by the popular press to this day.

How Much Do They Understand?

As the evidence mounts that the viewing of television by preschool children does not lead to significant learning gains, the question arises: how much do three- and four-year-olds actually understand of what they see on television? A number of studies of children's actual comprehension of television material find that while children clearly enjoy watching particular programs intended for their age group, and are thoroughly attentive while they watch, their understanding of what is happening on the screen is very small indeed.

In one study preschoolers' comprehension of an informational television program designed for their age group was measured by a standard evaluation procedure. A majority of the children understood less than half the tested information. Since the children who were asked some questions midway through the program segment showed no better comprehension than those who were asked all the questions at the end of the program, the possibility was eliminated that memory, not comprehension, was the deciding factor.[3]

In another study children aged 4, 7, and 10 years were shown a twenty-minute fairy tale of a kind commonly seen on television. After they saw the film the children's comprehension of the story was tested. Only 20 percent of the four-year-olds showed that they had understood the story line. The older children's comprehension was far superior. The authors conclude that "preschool children were unable to either remember what they had seen with any fidelity or to interpret accurately why the characters acted as they did."[4]

In a third study four-year-olds were shown a movie of a man performing a series of acts such as building a particular kind of block tower, putting a toy on top, and walking away. Twenty similar behaviors were shown in the film. The children were told before viewing that they would later be asked to do what the man did in the film. But the children did not learn the activities by watching them on film. They were able to reproduce only six of the twenty acts.

A second group of four-year-olds, however, who viewed the films in the company of an experimenter who *verbally described* each act as it was performed on the film demonstrated far greater comprehension, or at least retention, of the filmed material. These children showed a 50 percent increase in ability to correctly reenact the filmed activities.[5]

Parents, of course, have their own evidence of their young children's lack of comprehension: they see them engrossed in programs they cannot possibly understand.

A mother reports:

"My four-year-old loves and adores television and would watch it twenty-four hours a day if we let him. The other afternoon he watched the economic mini-summits on television, and you have to be some sort of nut if you sit there and watch those, *even if you understand them!*"

A father of a five-year old relates:

"My son and I were lying on the bed together the other night, watching a program about labor unrest in Cornwall, and he was absolutely fascinated. I said to him, 'Would you like me to explain this to you?' and he said, 'No Daddy, I'm just watching.'"

If watching "Sesame Street" does not bring about the same sort of cognitive gains that real-life linguistic experiences provide, and if young children spend thousands of hours engrossed in watching programs whose content they don't understand, what, then, *is* going on when they watch television? What sort of mental

"The rise in unemployment, however, which was somewhat offset by an expanding job market, was countered by an upturn in part-time dropouts, which, in turn, was diminished by seasonal factors, the anticipated summer slump, and, over-all, a small but perceptible rise in actual employment."

Drawing by Ed Arno; © 1975 The New Yorker Magazine, Inc.

activity are they engaging in while they watch television? And what effect might their involvement with this particular form of mental activity, so different from all other waking activities, have on their mental development?

Brain Hemispheres

When children want to know why they can't watch all the television they want, parents often resort to answers that suggest, with mock-humor, that too much television will have deleterious effects upon the brain. "It will turn your brains to mush" and "It will rot the brain" are phrases frequently used by parents trying to express their barely formed and unarticulated anxieties about the television experience.

The possible effects of heavy involvement with television on a child's brain development clearly do not lie in the direction of brain-rot or "brain-mush"; such a consequence would be amply apparent by now, and a generation of children raised watching television has come to maturity showing no signs of a downward trend in overall intelligence. And yet there *are* aspects of brain development that may be significantly affected by regular exposure to the television experience, though they cannot be measured by means of a simple IQ test. Some of these have to do with the particular ways in which the brain is organized to handle verbal and nonverbal material. An understanding of certain aspects of brain physiology may clarify the potential neurological impact of the television experience.

The cerebral cortex, that part of the brain responsible for the forms of higher thinking that distinguish human beings from lower animals, is not a single unit. It is composed of two separate hemispheres connected by a tangled mass of fibres. But unlike symmetrical organs such as the kidneys or lungs, in which each part is a precise duplicate of the other, each brain hemisphere has a number of unique and specialized functions. Each hemisphere controls the physical movements of the *opposite* side of the body; the left hemisphere, for instance, sends the signal that allows you to raise your right hand or move your right foot, while the right hemisphere controls all movements of the left side of the body.

But the most important distinction between the left and right hemispheres concerns the brain's control of verbal and nonverbal material. The left hemisphere, it has long been known, operates most of the brain's verbal and logical activities. For this reason it is often called the "dominant" hemisphere. The specific functions of the right hemisphere are less clearly understood, but it is known to be involved with spatial, visual, and perhaps affective activities. Thus it happens that when a person suffers a stroke in the left cerebral hemisphere, he is highly likely to lose all language capacity, while a right-hemisphere lesion will lead to a loss in face-recognition capacity, for instance, or shape-recognition ability, or in certain musical abilities such as tone recognition. After right-hemisphere surgery, patients may find it difficult to solve visual or tactile mazes, while patients undergoing similar operations on the left hemisphere perform well on such tests but show diminished abilities in verbal and mathematical tests.

Many of the evident dualities in human nature and the qualitative differences found in ways of mental functioning undoubtedly have their origins in the brain's peculiarly asymmetrical organization. There are two kinds of "intelligence," for instance, as tested on IQ tests—verbal-logical and spatial. Many people are disproportionately endowed with one or the other of these abilities. Such a discrepancy may well have a neurological basis.[6]

The clear division of human memory into two categories—verbal and visual—provides further support for the idea that there exist two discrete ways of thinking. Experimental evidence shows that the processes involved in remembering what we *see* are quite different from those by which we remember what we read or hear as words.[7] In everyday life this disparity is reflected in the common experience of recognizing the face of a person one has met before (visual memory), but failing to remember his name or even the circumstances under which the original meeting took place (verbal memory).

The phenomenon of *eidetic images,* those remarkable visual pictures that some children seem to retain in their mind's eye after looking at something, pictures that persist for many seconds or even minutes in so complete a form that they may be described in far greater detail than would be possible if the child were merely remembering, provides additional evidence that there is a verbal-visual dichotomy in the human brain. Researchers discovered that when those children gifted with an eidetic memory *verbalize* the material they are seeing—when, that is, they name or label a thing on their eidetic image—the named object vanishes instantly from the image.[8]

But hemisphere specialization, accompanied by two separate forms of mental organization, characterizes the adult brain alone. A very different situation obtains in regard to the brain of a young child.

The Transition Period

A child is not born with a brain in which each hemisphere serves a distinct and specialized function. At birth, of course, a baby does not possess any verbal abilities and therefore neither brain hemisphere may be characterized as the "dominant" or verbal one. Clearly a nonverbal form of mental functioning precedes the verbal in the child's early development, for long before the child acquires the use of language, he must employ some form of nonverbal "thought" in his daily life.

It is hard to conceive of what goes on in a child's mind before he learns to speak or understand words. Our own perception of thinking is so bound up with the notion of some sort of inner language that the nature of nonverbal thought is almost "unthinkable." And yet there is experimental evidence to prove its existence. Researchers have demonstrated that infants as young as three months of age can differentiate between pictures of a regular human face and a discrepant image, one, say, with three eyes.[9] Something akin to thinking must be going on as the infant compares the picture of the "wrong" face with his internalized experience of regular human faces. A "thought" of a regular, two-eyed human face must exist in the child's mind, an image unaccompanied by words (since the child is months away from language acquisition), and yet activated somehow by the discrepant image. This is how the child learns. Until the advent of language, he will continue to absorb experience by means of a nonverbal form of thought.

By the child's second birthday, language has usually become a dominant force in his life. The symbolic labeling of all objects and events dominates his mental efforts from this point on.

At the time the child begins to acquire language, each hemisphere of his cerebral cortex seems to be equally developed in verbal capacity. Researchers have learned, for instance, that lesions of the left hemisphere in children under the age of two are no more injurious to their future language development than lesions in the right hemisphere, whereas adults with similar injuries suffer permanent linguistic losses. Children with left-hemisphere damage occurring after the onset of language but before the age of four may suffer temporary linguistic difficulties, but in almost all cases language is quickly restored. Brain injuries incurred before the early teens also carry a good prognosis for recovery of language ability.

But when damage occurs after this critical period, the outlook is poor. Whatever disability has been suffered is generally permanent and irreparable. Since neurological evidence shows that it is around the age of 12 that the brain attains its final state of maturity in terms of structure and biochemistry, it appears that certain functions such as brain specialization lock into place at that time.

It is reasonable to assume that once language develops, the child's brain starts to specialize and verbal thinking begins to play an increasingly important role in his cognitive development. With the ability to speak and understand, the child becomes a more active participant in his thought and concept development, and nonverbal thinking ceases to serve its original function as the major source of learning. Now the child sets off on a journey of mental development that uniquely defines him as a human being—animals, after all, depend exclusively upon nonverbal forms of thinking.

But the organism's first form of mental functioning, that nonverbal mode of thinking in operation when an infant reacts with heightened attention to a three-eyed face, does not simply vanish when verbal thinking sets in. Undoubtedly the two forms of thinking continue to function side by side throughout life, each, however, under the aegis of a different hemisphere of the brain. Verbal thought is used whenever words, symbols, logic, or focal organization is required. Nonverbal functioning may be seen when the mind shifts into a qualitatively different state, as in those moments when one seems to be washed over by sensations unaccompanied by the usual mental manipulations or ratiocinations. Staring into a flickering fireplace is an example of a nonverbal form of mental operation: the mind perceives the changing movements of the flames —the visual stimuli are obviously received by the brain's sense receptors—and yet no verbal manipulations occur. A mode of mental functioning that requires nothing but intake and acceptance is in operation.

Brain Changes

If during the child's formative years when the brain is in transition from its original, unspecialized state to one in which each hemisphere takes on a specific function the child engages in a repeated and time-consuming nonverbal, primarily visual activity—if, in effect, he receives excessive stimulation for the right-hemisphere forms of mental functioning—might this not have a discernible effect on his neurological development?

This question requires consideration because there are reasons to believe that television viewing is essentially such a nonverbal, visual experience in the lives on young children. The trancelike state that characterizes many children's viewing behavior suggests that normal, active cognition is temporarily replaced by a state of mind more akin to meditation or other right-hemisphere—mediated states. The use of television, moreover, as a pacifying agent, a relaxant for overstimulated children and a sedative for troublesome children, points up the nonverbal nature of the television experience.

Further evidence of the nonverbal effect of children's television experiences is seen in television's failure to act as an adequate replacement for real-life linguistic opportunities. The director of a Harlem center for deprived preschool children reports that child after child arrives at his school virtually mute, unable to speak a single intelligible sentence, although medical examinations reveal no clinical deficiencies, either physical or mental. "It is usually diagnosed as a speech defect," he observes, "but most often I have found it to be simply the result of hearing bad English, listening to nothing but television, and being spoken to hardly at all . . ."[10]

If those thousands and thousands of hours young children spend viewing television *did* serve as a source of verbal stimulation and *did* help to develop the verbal centers of the brain, if all those fine adult words and phrases coming out of the television set did function as effectively as real-life talking and listening, then surely a generation capable of expressing itself elegantly and clearly would have emerged. This does not appear to be the case. Indeed, in a look at the "television generation" later in these pages, it will become clear that a serious diminution of verbal abilities has occurred among those children who grew up watching great quantities of television.

Why does a child who listens to "nothing but television" find no profit from his television exposure? It must be that there is a critical difference between a language experience that requires no reciprocal participation and one in which the child must involve himself actively, as in an exchange with another person. And if the child's television viewing indeed involves a different sort of mental activity than his real-life experiences, this activity may prove to stimulate different parts of his developing brain.

Just as the lungs of a chain smoker are demonstrably different from a nonsmoker's lungs, is it not possible that the brain of a twelve-year-old who has spent ten thousand hours in a darkened room watching moving images on a small screen is in specific ways different from the brain of a child who has watched little or no television? Might not the television child emerge from childhood with certain left-hemisphere skills—those verbal and logical ones—less developed than the visual and spatial capabilities governed by the right hemisphere?

In considering these questions two preliminary questions must be raised: Does experience of *any* sort affect brain development? And if so, does early experience carry more weight than events that occur in the later stages of development?

Until quite recently the question of whether any experience at all is capable of producing actual changes within the brain was a subject of controversy and speculation. While some scientists believed that the *use* of cells furthered their development, and thus that environmental stimulation would necessarily influence a child's cerebral development, others felt that brain capacity and development were genetically predetermined and unaffected by the events and experiences of life.

As a result of recent experiments investigating brain changes in animals raised in impoverished environments (bare cages, with little outside stimulation) compared with changes in animals raised in enriched environments (cages filled with toys and equipment, and numerous opportunities to engage in stimulating activities), there can no longer be any doubt that many aspects of brain anatomy and chemistry *are* changed by stimulation. These experiments demonstrated an increase in weight of the cerebral cortex as well as an increased activity of brain enzymes in those animals raised in enriched environments as compared to those deprived of stimulation.[11] Such an increase in cortical weight and enzyme activity is an indication of increased mental capacity.

While it is difficult to draw direct conclusions about human experience from animal experiments, there is a body of human evidence that supports the findings of these animal experiments and invites their application to humans. This evidence is found in studies of infants and young children reared in sterile hospital wards, orphanages, and other institutions, all as impoverished in terms of mental stimulation as the bare cages of the rats in the animal experiments.[12] Though the brains of these deprived children cannot, of course, be examined for physical and chemical changes, assumptions can be made about the effects of an understimulated environment upon human brain development on the basis of the children's observed behavior and testable mental abilities. Since these children invariably proved to be severely retarded when tested and compared to children raised in families or even in institutions providing a more stimulating environment, and since it is known that they were not mentally deficient to begin with, it is not farfetched to suppose that their mental retardation was accompanied by, or resulted from, actual changes in brain physiology, and that these changes were caused by environmental understimulation.

There is another body of evidence suggesting that the experiences of the early years, when the organism is growing and developing most rapidly, have a *greater* effect on brain development than those occurring in later years. One of many such experiments demonstrating the importance of early environmental stimulation was performed in recent years with kittens as the experimental subjects:

The eyes of newborn kittens were stitched together to prevent them from seeing. By this means the kittens were kept in darkness for three months. When the animals' eyes were opened, the researchers discovered that the kittens did not proceed to acquire normal vision as they would have done a few days after birth. In the absence of normal visual experiences within the first months of life, the kittens' visual system proved to be permanently damaged—the brain center responsible for vision did not function properly, for some reason. However, when the eyes of older kittens who had already acquired normal vision, or of adult cats, were artificially closed for an equal period of time, no optical damage resulted.[13] Other experiments with chimpanzees support the theory that in the early stages of an organism's development there are sensitive periods of growth during which the presence or absence of certain experiences is critical for normal brain development.[14]

Among humans recent large-scale early education programs for infants and very young children are beginning to demonstrate that early and persistent enrichment can lead to permanent gains in mental ability.[15] And conversely, social evidence suggests that the deficits of an environmentally impoverished early childhood cannot be later undone by remedial programs and opportunities for mental stimulation.[16] (The disappointing impact of the Head Start program is one of a number of indications that the cognitive die is cast, as it were, before the fifth or sixth year.)

Yet another proof of the importance of early stimulation is found in the cases of so-called feral children, those survivors of an early childhood deprived of all human contact. Writing of these children, who are commonly presumed to have been raised by animals, the linguist Maurice Merleau-Ponty notes:

> There is a period during which a child is particularly sensitive to language and during which he can learn to talk. It has been shown that if a child . . . is not in an environment in which there are people who talk, then he will never be able to talk with the same ease as those who have learned to speak during the period in question.[17]

A Commitment to Language

Given the evidence that environmental experience affects brain development in definable, measurable ways, and that early experience is more influential than later experience, it seems inevitable that the television experience, which takes up so many hours of a child's waking day, must have some effects upon his brain development. And yet children's brains cannot be dissected and examined to satisfy a scientist's curiosity. Nor can animal experiments cast reliable light on questions dealing with mental functions peculiar to the human species, such as thinking or verbalizing.

Nevertheless, the fact that the brain of a young child is different in important ways from an adult brain may help us to localize the areas of neurological impact of the television experience. For it will be in those *changing* areas that any neurological change will presumably occur.

Such an area of difference between the child's and the adult's brain is precisely that of brain-hemisphere specialization, and the balance that exists between verbal and nonverbal forms of mental organization. It is here that the television experience may prove to have its greatest impact.

This is not to suggest that television viewing will prevent a normal child from learning to speak. Only in cases of gross deprivation where children are almost totally isolated from human sounds will they not proceed according to a fairly universal language-learning schedule and fail to acquire the rudiments of speech.

It is not the child's actual acquisition of language but his *commitment* to language as a means of expression and to the verbal mode as the ultimate source of fulfillment that is at stake, a commitment that may have a physiological basis in the balance of right- and left-hemisphere development.

For a young child in the process of developing those basic mental structures, concepts, and understandings required to achieve his highest potential as a rational human being, a child who has only recently made the transition from nonverbal to verbal thought, much depends upon his opportunities to exercise his growing verbal skills. The greater the child's verbal opportunities, the greater the likelihood that his language will grow in complexity and his rational, verbal thinking abilities will sharpen. The fewer his opportunities, the greater the likelihood that certain linguistic areas will remain undeveloped or underdeveloped as critical time periods come and go.

To a grown-up, nonverbal mental activities carry connotations of relaxation from the ardors of normal logical thinking and promise a much-sought-after achievement of peace and serenity. But to a young child in his formative, language-learning years, any extended regression into nonverbal mental functioning such as the television experience offers must be seen as a potential setback. As the child takes in television words and images hour after hour, day after day, with little of the mental effort that forming his own thoughts and feelings and molding them into words would require, as he *relaxes* year after year, a pattern emphasizing nonverbal cognition becomes established.

For unlike the tired businessman or professional woman or harried housewife who turns on the television set to "unwind," the young child has a built-in need for mental activity. He is a learning machine, an "absorbent mind," a glutton for experience. In a culture that depends upon a precise and effective use of spoken and written language, his optimal development requires not merely adequate, but abundant opportunities to manipulate, to learn, to synthesize experience. It is his parents, fatigued by his incessant demands for learning in the broadest sense of the word (learning that may involve whining, screaming, throwing things, pestering), who require the "relaxation" afforded by setting him before the television screen and causing him to become, once again, the passive captive of his own sensations he was when nonverbal thought was his only means of learning.

5

Television and Reading

Until the television era a young child's access to symbolic representations of reality was limited. Unable to read, he entered the world of fantasy primarily by way of stories told to him or read to him from a book. But rarely did such "literary" experiences take up a significant proportion of a child's waking time; even when a willing reader or storyteller was available, an hour or so a day was more time than most children spent ensconced in the imagination of others. And when the pre-television child *did* enter those imaginary worlds, he always had a grown-up escort along to interpret, explain, and comfort, if need be. Before he learned to read, it was difficult for the child to enter the fantasy world alone.

For this reason the impact of television was undoubtedly greater on preschoolers and pre-readers than on any other group. By means of television, very young children were able to enter and spend sizable portions of their waking time in a secondary world of incorporeal people and intangible things, unaccompanied, in too many cases, by an adult guide or comforter. School-age children fell into a different category. Because they could read, they had other opportunities to leave reality behind. For these children television was merely *another* imaginary world.

But since reading, once the school child's major imaginative experience, has now been virtually eclipsed by television, the television experience must be compared with the reading experience to try to discover whether they are, indeed, similar activities fulfilling similar needs in a child's life.

54

What Happens When You Read

It is not enough to compare television watching and reading from the viewpoint of quality. Although the quality of the material available in each medium varies enormously, from junky books and shoddy programs to literary masterpieces and fine, thoughtful television shows, the *nature* of the two experiences is different and that difference significantly affects the impact of the material taken in.

Few people besides linguistics students and teachers of reading are aware of the complex mental manipulations involved in the reading process. Shortly after learning to read, a person assimilates the process into his life so completely that the words in books seem to acquire an existence almost equal to the objects or acts they represent. It requires a fresh look at a printed page to recognize that those symbols that we call letters of the alphabet are completely abstract shapes bearing no inherent "meaning" of their own. Look at an "o," for instance, or a "k." The "o" is a curved figure; the "k" is an intersection of three straight lines. Yet it is hard to divorce their familiar figures from their sounds, though there is nothing "o-ish" about an "o" or "k-ish" about "k." A reader unfamiliar with the Russian alphabet will find it easy to look at the symbol "ш" and see it as an abstract shape; a Russian reader will find it harder to detach that symbol from its sound, *shch*. And even when trying to consider "k" as an abstract symbol, we cannot see it without the feeling of a "k" sound somewhere between the throat and the ears, a silent pronunciation of "k" that occurs the instant we see the letter.

That is the beginning of reading: we learn to transform abstract figures into sounds, and groups of symbols into the combined sounds that make up the words of our language. As the mind transforms the abstract symbols into sounds and the sounds into words, it "hears" the words, as it were, and thereby invests them with meanings previously learned in the spoken language.[1] Invariably, as the skill of reading develops, the meaning of each word begins to seem to dwell within those symbols that make up the word. The word "dog," for instance, comes to bear some relationship with the real animal. Indeed, the word "dog" seems to *be* a dog in a certain sense, to possess some of the qualities of a dog. But it is only as a result of a swift and complex series of mental activities that the word "dog" is transformed from a series of meaningless squiggles into an idea of something real. This process goes on smoothly and continuously as we read, and yet it becomes no less complex. The brain must carry out all the steps of decoding and investing with meaning each time we read; but it becomes more adept at it as the skill develops, so that we lose the sense of struggling with symbols and meanings that children have when they first learn to read.

But not merely does the mind *hear* words in the process of reading; it is important to remember that reading involves images as well. For when the reader sees the word "dog" and understands the idea of "dog," an image representing a dog is conjured up as well. The precise nature of this "reading image" is little understood, nor is there agreement about what relation it bears to visual images taken in directly by the eyes. Nevertheless images necessarily color our reading, else we would perceive no meaning, merely empty words. The great difference between these "reading images" and the images we take in when viewing television is this: we *create* our own images when reading, based upon our own life experiences and reflecting our own individual needs, while we must accept what we receive when watching television images. This aspect of reading, which might be called "creative" in the narrow sense of the word, is present during all reading experiences, regardless of *what* is being read. The reader "creates" his own images as he reads, almost as if he were creating his own, small, inner television program. The result is a nourishing experience for the imagination. As Bruno Bettelheim notes, "Television captures the imagination but does not liberate it. A good book at once stimulates and frees the mind."[2]

Television images do not go through a complex symbolic transformation. The mind does not have to decode and manipulate during the television experience. Perhaps this is a reason why the visual images received directly from a television set are strong, stronger, it appears, than the images conjured up mentally while reading. But ultimately they satisfy less. A ten-year-old child reports on the effects of seeing television dramatizations of books he has previously read: "The TV people leave a stronger impression. Once you've seen a character on TV, he'll always look like that in your mind, even if you made a different picture of him in your mind before, when you read the book yourself." And yet, as the same child reports, "the thing about a book is that you have so much freedom. You can make each character look exactly the way you want him to look. You're more in control of things when you read a book than when you see something on TV."

It may be that television-bred children's reduced opportunities to indulge in this "inner picture-making" accounts for the curious inability of so many children today to adjust to nonvisual experiences. This is commonly reported by experienced teachers who bridge the gap between the pretelevision and the television eras.

"When I read them a story without showing them pictures, the children always complain—'I can't see.' Their attention flags," reports a first-grade teacher. "They'll begin to talk or wander off. I have to really work to develop their visualizing skills. I tell them that there's nothing to see, that the story is coming out of my mouth, and that they can make their own pictures in their 'mind's eye.' They get better at visualizing, with practice. But children never needed to learn how to visualize before television, it seems to me."

Viewing vs. Reading: Concentration

Because reading demands complex mental manipulations, a reader is required to concentrate far more than a telvision viewer. An audio expert notes that "with the electronic media it is openness [that counts]. Openness permits auditory and visual stimuli more direct access to the brain . . . someone who is taught to concentrate will fail to perceive many patterns of information conveyed by the electronic stimuli."[8]

It may be that a predisposition toward concentration, acquired, perhaps, through one's reading experiences, makes one an inadequate television watcher. But it seems far more likely that the reverse situation obtains: that a predisposition toward "openness" (which may be understood to mean the opposite of focal concentration), acquired through years and years of television viewing, has influenced adversely viewers' ability to concentrate, to read, to write clearly—in short, to demonstrate any of the verbal skills a literate society requires.

Pace

A comparison between reading and viewing may be made in respect to the pace of each experience, and the relative control a person has over that pace, for the pace may influence the ways one uses the material received in each experience. In addition, the pace of each experience may determine how much it intrudes upon other aspects of one's life.

The pace of reading, clearly, depends entirely upon the reader. He may read as slowly or as rapidly as he can or wishes to read. If he does not understand something, he may stop and reread it, or go in search of elucidation before continuing. The reader can accelerate his pace when the material is easy or less than interesting, and slow down when it is difficult or enthralling. If what he reads is moving, he can put down the book for a few moments and cope with his emotions without fear of losing anything.

The pace of the television experience cannot be controlled by the viewer; only its beginning and end are within his control as he clicks the knob on and off. He cannot slow down a delightful program or speed up a dreary one. He cannot "turn back" if a word or phrase is not understood. The program moves inexorably forward, and what is lost or misunderstood remains so.

Nor can the television viewer readily transform the material he receives into a form that might suit his particular emotional needs, as he invariably does with material he reads. The images move too quickly. He cannot use his own imagination to invest the people and events portrayed on television with the personal meanings that would help him understand and resolve relationships and conflicts in his own life; he is under the power of the imagination of the show's creators. In the television experience the eyes and ears are overwhelmed with the immediacy of sights and sounds. They flash from the television set just fast enough for the eyes and ears to take them in before moving on quickly to the new pictures and sounds ... so as *not to lose the thread*.

Not to lose the thread ... it is this need, occasioned by the irreversible direction and relentless velocity of the television experience, that not only limits the workings of the viewer's imagination, but also causes television to intrude into human affairs far more than reading experiences can ever do. If someone enters the room while one is watching television—a friend, a relative, a child, someone, perhaps, one has not seen for some time—one must continue to watch or one will lose the thread. The greetings must wait, for the television program will not. A book, of course, can be set aside, with a pang of regret, perhaps, but with no sense of permanent loss.

A grandparent describes a situation that is, by all reports, not uncommon:

"Sometimes when I come to visit the girls, I'll walk into their room and they're watching a TV program. Well, I know they love me, but it makes me feel *bad* when I tell them hello, and they say, without even looking up, 'Wait a minute . . . we have to see the end of this program.' It hurts me to have them care more about that machine and those little pictures than about being glad to see me. I know that they probably can't help it, but still. . . ."

Can they help it? Ultimately the power of a television viewer to release himself from his viewing in order to attend to human demands arising in the course of his viewing is not altogether a function of the pace of the program. After all, the viewer might *choose* to operate according to human priorities, rather than electronic dictatorship. He might quickly decide "to hell with this program" and simply stop watching when a friend entered the room or a child needed attention.

He might . . . but the hypnotic power of television makes it difficult to shift one's attention away, makes one desperate not to lose the thread of the program.

Why Is It So Hard to Stop Watching?

A number of perceptual factors unique to the television experience may play a role in making television more *fascinating* than any other vicarious experience, factors to do with the nature of the electronic images on the screen and the ways the eye takes them in.[4]

Whereas in real life we perceive but a tiny part of the visual panorama around us with the fovea, the sharp-focusing part of the eye, taking in the rest of the world with our fuzzy peripheral vision, when we watch television we take in the entire frame of an image with our sharp foveal vision. Let us say that the image on the television screen depicts a whole room or a mountain landscape; if we were there in real life, we would be able to perceive only a very small part of the room or the landscape clearly with any single glance. On television, however, we can see the entire picture sharply. Our peripheral vision is not involved in viewing that scene; indeed, as the eye focuses upon the television screen and takes it all in sharply, the mind blots out the peripheral world entirely. Since in real life the periphery distracts and diffuses our attention, this absence of periphery must serve to abnormally heighten our attention to the television image.

Another unique feature of the television image is the remarkable activity of all contours on the television screen. While the normal contours of real-life objects and people are stationary, the electronic mechanism that creates images on a screen produces contours that are ever moving, although the viewer is hardly aware of the movement. Since the eye is drawn to fixate more strongly on moving than on stationary objects, one result of the activity of television contours is to make them more attention-binding.

Yet another consequence is to make the eye defocus slightly when fixing its attention on the television screen. The reason is this: in viewing television the steadily changing visual activity of the contour causes the eye to have difficulties in fixating properly. Now in real life when the eye does not fixate properly a signal is sent to the visual center of the brain, which then takes corrective steps. Since improper fixation is normally the result of an eye tremor or some physical dysfunction of the viewer himself rather than of the thing being viewed, the visual system will attempt to make corrections in the eye tremor or in some part of the viewer's visual system. However, in viewing television, it is the visual activity *at the contour of the image* that is causing the difficulties in fixation. Thus the visual system will have increasing difficulty in maintaining its normal fixation. Therefore it may be easier to give up striving for a perfect, focused fixation on a television picture, and to accommodate by a somewhat defocused fixation.

The sensory confusion that occurs as a result of the activity of television images is not unlike the state that occurs when the semi-circular canals of the ears, which serve to maintain our balance and help the brain make the necessary adjustments to the body's movements, are confused by motion from external sources (as when a person stands still and yet his ear canals are moved this way and that by the motion of a car or ship or airplane). The unpleasant symptoms of sea-sickness or carsickness reflect this internal confusion.

The slight defocusing of the eyes while viewing tele-vision, while not as unpleasant as seasickness (it is barely perceptible, in fact), may nevertheless have subtle consequences that serve to make the television experience more dysfunctional for the organism than other experiences such as reading. Research shows that defocusing of the eyes normally accompanies various fantasy and day-dreaming states. Thus the ma-terial perceived on television may take on an air of unreality, a dreamlike quality. Moreover, similar vis-ual-motor conflicts are frequently described as features of many drug experiences by users. This may very well be a reason for the trancelike nature of so many view-ers' television experience, and may help to explain why the television image has so strong and hypnotic a fas-cination. It has been suggested that "early experiences with electronic displays are predisposing to later en-joyment of psychoactive drugs which produce similar perceptual effects."[5]

All these perceptual anomalies may conspire to fas-cinate the viewer and glue him to the television set.

Of course there are variations in the attention-get-ting and attention-sustaining powers of television im-ages, many of which depend on such factors as the amount of movement present on the screen at any given moment, and the velocity of change from image to image. It is a bit chilling to consider that the pro-ducers of the most influential program for preschool children, "Sesame Street," employed modern technol-ogy in the form of a "distractor" machine to test each segment of their program to ensure that it would cap-ture and hold the child's attention to the highest degree possible. With the help of the "distractor," the makers of "Sesame Street" found that the fast-paced cartoons, and fast-moving stories were most effective in sustain-ing a child's attention. This attitude toward young children and their television experiences may well be compared to that revealed by Monica Sims of the BBC who states: "We're not trying to tie children to the television screen. If they go away and play halfway through our programs, that's fine."[6]

The Basic Building Blocks

There is another difference between reading and television viewing that must affect the response to each experience. This is the relative acquaintance of readers and viewers with the fundamental elements of each medium. While the reader is familiar with the basic building blocks of the reading medium, the television viewer has little acquaintance with those of the television medium.

As a person reads, he has his own writing experience to fall back upon. His understanding of what he reads, and his feelings about it, are necessarily affected, and deepened, by his possession of writing as a means of communicating. As a child begins to learn reading, he begins to acquire the rudiments of writing. That these two skills are always acquired together is important and not coincidental. As the child learns to read words, he needs to understand that a word is something he can write himself, though his muscle control may temporarily prevent him from writing it clearly. That he wields such power over the words he is struggling to decipher makes the reading experience a satisfying one right from the start.

A young child watching television enters a realm of materials completely beyond his control—and understanding. Though the images that appear on the screen may be reflections of familiar people and things, they appear as if by magic. The child cannot create similar images, nor even begin to understand how those flickering, electronic shapes and forms come into being. He takes on a far more powerless and ignorant role in front of the television set than in front of a book.

There is no doubt that many young children have a confused relationship to the television medium. When a group of preschool children were asked, "How do kids get to be on your TV?" only 22 percent of them showed any real comprehension of the nature of the television images. When asked, "Where do the people and kids and things go when your TV is turned off?" only 20 percent of the three-year-olds showed the smallest glimmer of understanding. Although there was an increase in comprehension among the four-year-olds, the authors of the study note that "even among the older children the vast majority still did not grasp the nature of television pictures."[7]

The child's feelings of power and competence are nourished by another feature of the reading experience that does not obtain for television: the nonmechanical, easily accessible, and easily transportable nature of reading matter. The child can always count on a book for pleasure, though the television set may break down at a crucial moment. The child may take a book with him wherever he goes, to his room, to the park, to his friend's house, to school to read under his desk: he can *control* his use of books and reading materials. The television set is stuck in a certain place; it cannot be moved easily. It certainly cannot be casually transported from place to place by a child. The child must not only watch television wherever the set is located, but he must watch certain programs at certain times, and is powerless to change what comes out of the set and when it comes out.

In this comparison of reading and television experiences a picture begins to emerge that quite confirms the commonly held notion that reading is somehow "better" than television viewing. Reading involves a complex form of mental activity, trains the mind in concentration skills, develops the powers of imagination and inner visualization; the flexibility of its pace lends itself to a better and deeper comprehension of the material communicated. Reading engrosses, but does not hypnotize or seduce the reader from his human responsibilities. Reading is a two-way process: the reader can also write; television viewing is a one-way street: the viewer cannot create television images. And books are ever available, ever controllable. Television controls.

A Preference for Watching

There would be little purpose in comparing the experiences of reading and television viewing if it were not for the incontrovertible fact that children's viewing experiences influence their reading in critical ways, affecting *how much* they read, *what* they read, how they *feel* about reading, and, since writing skills are closely related to reading experiences, what they write and how well they write.

There is no doubt that children read fewer books when television is available to them. A child is more likely to turn on the television set when he has nothing to do than to pick up a book to read. (In a survey of over 500 fourth- and fifth-graders, all subjects showed a preference for *watching* over reading contents of any kind.[8]) This is partly if not entirely because reading requires greater mental activity and it is human nature to opt for an entertainment that requires less effort rather than more.

Children candidly reveal this tendency when speaking of their television viewing:

"I mean television, you don't have to worry about getting really bored because it's happening and you don't have to do any work to see it, to have it happen. But you have to work to read, and that's no fun. I mean, it's fun when it's a good book, but how can you tell if the book will be good? Anyhow, I'd rather see it as a television program," allows the twelve-year-old daughter of a college English teacher.

Parents confirm the trend. The mother of boys aged 12 and 10 and a girl aged 9 reports:

"My children have trouble finding books they like in the library. They seem to have some sort of resistance to books, even though my husband and I are avid readers. I think if they didn't have television available they'd calmly spend more time looking for something good in the library. They'd *have* to, to avoid boredom. But now they don't really *look* in the library, whenever I take them. They don't zero in on anything.

It's not the ultimate entertainment for them, reading. There's always something better and easier to do. So they don't have to look hard at the library. They just zip through quickly and hardly ever find more than one or two books that interest them enough to take out."

Those children who have difficulty with reading are even more likely to combat boredom by turning to television than successful readers. Television plays a profoundly negative role in such children's intellectual development, since it is only by reading a great deal that they can hope to overcome their reading problems. This point is frequently raised by teachers and reading specialists when discussing the effects of television viewing on children's reading. Television watching does not prevent normal children from acquiring reading skills (although it may cause them to read less), but it does seem to compound the problems of children with reading disabilities because it offers them a pleasurable nonverbal alternative and thus reduces their willingness to work at reading in order to find vicarious pleasures.

That it is the availability of television that reduces the amount of reading children do rather than some other factor is easily demonstrated. In the absence of a television set—when the set is temporarily broken, or when the family has eliminated television entirely—a universal increase in reading, both by parents and by children, is reported. When the less taxing mental activity is unavailable, children turn to reading for entertainment, more willing to put up with the "work" involved.

Lazy Readers

Besides reducing children's *need* to read and, by occupying so many hours of their day, their opportunities for reading, the television experience may subtly affect the actual *ways* in which children read, what might be called their reading style. For while children of the television era still read, and read with pleasure, something about their reading has changed.

A speaker at a recent conference of educators discussed a new phenomenon she referred to as the "lazy reader." This is an intelligent child from a highly-educated family who has somehow never made the transition from the acquisition of the reading skill to an ability to absorb what he reads. Critic George Steiner refers to this sort of reader when he notes: "A large majority of those who have passed through the primary and secondary school system can 'read' but not *read*."[9] Teachers seem to be encountering more of these "lazy readers" every year.

The "lazy reader" reads well, but not attentively, that is, not with the degree of involvement and concentration required for full comprehension. Concentration, after all, is a skill that requires practice to develop; the television child's opportunities to learn to focus attention sharply and sustain concentration are limited. Indeed, the mental diffuseness demanded by the television experience may cause children who have logged thousands of hours in front of the set to enter the reading world more superficially, more impatiently, more vaguely.

Educator Donald Barr refers to this sort of reader when he writes: "Children may pick up and leaf through more books, but what they do looks to me less and less like reading every year." He, too, connects the deterioration in reading with children's television experiences. "TV stimulates casting your eye over the page, and that is a far different thing from reading."[10]

Nonbooks

If children are reading in ways that differ subtly from pre-television reading styles, how does this change affect *what* they choose to read? There are indeed indications that a change has occurred in children's reading preferences, with different kinds of books being read for pleasure than in the days before children watched television. Part of this change may result from the *contents* of the television programs children watch. For instance, the notable decline in the popularity of fiction among children in the last two decades seems related to the fantasy material available to them on television.[11] But other changes in children's reading interests may be related to the influences of the actual television *experience* upon their reading style.

The headmaster of a selective boys' school in New York reports: "For as much television as our boys watch I have found no substantial correlation between the amount of television watching and the circulation of books from the library. The important change is in the *kinds* of books the boys read. There has been a declining interest in fantasy, adventure—fiction of all sorts. But what is really a new trend, it seems to me, is the great interest children have in reading the 'nonbook' kind of thing. The most conspicuous example of a 'nonbook' is the *Guinness Book of Records.* A great deal of the reading the boys seem to be doing these days falls into that category."

The nonbook seems designed to accommodate a new reading style. It is not the kind of book with a sustained story or a carefully developed argument that is read from beginning to end. A book to be scanned, read in fits and starts, skimmed, requiring little concentration, focused thinking, or inner visualization, it provides enough information or visually pleasing material to divert the child who does not feel comfortable with the old sequential style of reading. The ultimate nonbook, of course, is one that not only does without a consecutive story but also eliminates words entirely. The increasingly pictorial nature of so many books for adults and children suggests that such a trend has already begun. (Comic books fall into a similar category, but they have never been considered "real" books). A case in point is the *manga genśho,* or cartoon phenomenon, that has begun to sweep the Japanese publishing industry, with long lists of new paperback cartoon books with few words flooding the book market. A Japanese publisher notes: "This mindless cartoon phenomenon is all part of the developing postcard culture. We are shifting from a culture of readers to one of watchers."[12]

An important aspect of the nonbook for the television-bred child is its instant accessibility. There is no need to struggle with "getting into" a nonbook, a process in which the reader must make the transition from his own reality to the world of the book. This initial stage is often confusing, as new names and places appear and a host of new characters are introduced. But the reader perseveres with the knowledge that he will soon be safely settled into the book and commence to enjoy it.

There is no equivalent "getting into" process in viewing a television program. Although a certain amount of confusion about names and characters may also exist at the start of a television experience, the program moves on with far less effort required from the viewer to unsort and imagine and understand. The physical world of the television program is immediately available to the eye—no taxing descriptions of people or places need be endured before the action moves on. And the visial material and sounds fill the eyes and ears so completely that there is little opportunity for the mind to wander and become discouraged.

Like television, a nonbook makes no stretching demands at the start. Composed of tiny facts and snippets of interesting material, it does not change in any way during the course of a child's involvement in it. It does not get easier, or harder, or more exciting, or more suspenseful; it remains the same. Thus there is no need to "get into" a nonbook because there are no further stages to progress to. But while the reader of a nonbook is spared the trouble of difficult entry into a vicarious world, he is also denied the deep satisfactions that reading *real* books may provide.

Parents often assuage their anxieties about their children's television involvement by insisting that their children still read. But the reading that parents report often falls into this very category of nonbooks.

"Andrew loves TV but he does still read, you know. He reads a great deal for information. He loves to look things up and so on. But he finds most fiction boring, or biographies or books like that. But he does read well, you know, so I don't worry as much."

"Writing Is Book Talk"

A corollary of the decline in reading skills since the mid-1960s is a similar, if not even more pronounced, deterioration in *writing* skills of American students: "Plagued by increasing numbers of students who are unable to write coherent sentences or handle simple arithmetic, more and more colleges and universities are finding they have to offer remedial work in such basic skills," begins an article in *The New York Times*.[13]

According to the National Assessment of Educational Progress, the writing performance of American students has been steadily deteriorating. The majority of students tend to use only the simplest sentence structure and the most elementary vocabulary when they write. The essays of thirteen- to seventeen-year-olds are far more awkward, incoherent, and disorganized today than the writings of teen-agers of previous decades.[14] The connection between television's effects on children's reading abilities and the decline in their writing skills is clear: there is no question in the minds of educators that a student who cannot read with true comprehension will never learn to write well. "Writing, after all, is book talk," says a teacher of language education, "and you only learn book talk by reading."

A high school English teacher observes:

"There is no question that your success as a student depends enormously on your vocabulary, both in what you can understand as you read and in how you reason as you write, and there is *no way* to build up a good vocabulary except by reading—there just is none."

"Learning to write," says Carlos Baker, author and educator, "is the hardest, most important thing any child does. Learning to write is learning to think."[15]

Professor Baker undoubtedly refers to the logical, verbal kind of thinking that is required for intellectual efforts. For such work the skills involved in learning to write effectively are surely necessary. But a child can learn other ways of thinking, those characterized by rapid scanning and visual receptivity. Learning to write well will not encourage this nonverbal form of thinking, nor, conversely, will nonverbal thinking be helpful in acquiring writing skills. Quite the contrary, the two work at cross-purposes. It is, however, nonverbal thinking that is nurtured by television watching.

The role television has played in the national decline of reading and writing skills has not been precisely assessed—perhaps it never can be. But the nonverbal nature of the television experience, and the great involvement of children with television from their earliest years to the end of their school careers, makes a connection between television watching and inadequate writing skills seem inevitable. In this regard, one of America's most skillful writers, E. B. White, says, "Short of throwing away all the television sets, I really don't know what we can do about writing."[16]

Perhaps the decline in reading and writing abilities of high school and college students today has occurred because certain basic verbal learnings usually acquired through reading have been neglected as a result of television watching.

"So many of my students can't seem to *hear* when a sentence should end or where a semicolon should go as against where a comma should go," states a professor of English at a Midwestern university. "It's not a physical loss. Their ears hear words. But the mechanism that recognizes 'a complete thought' and distinguishes it from 'an incomplete thought' seems to be missing. Their thinking doesn't seem to have a subject-verb structure built into it, and they are not able to measure incoming sentences against that subject-verb structure and either declare that they need a period at the end or that they mustn't have a period at the end. And mind you, these are bright students. There's nothing wrong with their thinking. It's just different in certain ways."

In comparing viewing with reading, the final question must be this: Is there, ultimately, a *need* for reading in human lives? Though the television experience fulfills

Why Books?

different needs and involves different modes of thinking, still might it not reflect a change in people's needs and ways of thinking that will prevail in the future? Is there something a bit old-fashioned and rigid, perhaps even reactionary, about a defense of reading in the television era?

The answer must lie in the relationship of each medium to the humanity of its audience. In reading, a person utilizes his most unique human ability: verbal thinking. He transforms the symbols on the page into a particular form dictated by his own human nature, his wishes, fears, and inner needs. As novelist Jerzy Kosinski has noted, reading "offers unexpected, unchannelled associations, new insights into the tides and drifts of one's own life. The reader is tempted to venture beyond a text, to contemplate his own life in light of the book's personalized meanings."[17]

In the television experience a viewer is carried along by the exigencies of a mechanical device, unable to bring into play his most highly developed mental abilities or to fulfill his individual emotional needs. He is entertained while watching television, but his passive participation leaves him unchanged in a human sense. For while television viewing provides diversion, reading allows and supports growth.

6

Television and Violence: a New Approach

Searching for a Link

The subject of television violence and its potential effect on children has long been a source of controversy. Congressional studies were carried out in 1954, 1961, 1964, and 1970. When the Surgeon General's *Report on Television and Social Behavior* was published in 1972, four of the five volumes were devoted to studies dealing with the effects of viewing violent television programs. Indeed, most seminars, articles, and studies considering the effects of television on children focus on this single issue.

The intense interest in the effects of television violence upon children is understandable: the number of juveniles arrested for serious and violent crimes increased *1600 percent* between the years 1952 and 1972, according to FBI figures.[1] Since this is the very period in which television became ascendant in the lives of American children, and since the programs children watch are saturated with crime and destruction, it has long seemed reasonable to search for a link between the two.

And yet this link continues to elude social scientists and researchers, in spite of their great efforts to demonstrate its existence. The truly repugnant, sadistic, amazingly various violence appearing on home screens must surely have subtle effects upon children's behavior, but it clearly does not cause them to behave in seriously antisocial ways. After all, the majority of American children are regularly exposed to those violent programs that have been proposed as a causative factor in the increase of juvenile violence, and yet the children involved in the FBI statistics are but a small proportion of the viewing population. And while a number of research studies *do* indicate a relationship between viewing violence on television and subsequent aggressive behavior, that behavior as seen in the research laboratory obviously does not involve rape or murder, the serious crimes included in the FBI report, but rather ordinary childish aggression—pushing, shoving, hitting, and so on.

Common sense balks at the idea that television violence will lead normal children to become juvenile delinquents. Indeed, it is the intuitive certainty that watching violent programs will not turn their children into rapists and murderers that permits parents to be lax about their children's indulgence in their favorite, invariably violent, programs in spite of the earnest advice of psychologists and educators.

It is particularly hard for parents to buy the idea that television instigates aggressive behavior when its function in the home is so different. There, television keeps children quiet and passive, cuts down on loud and boisterous play, prevents outbursts between brothers and sisters, and eliminates a number of potentially destructive household "experiments" children might be indulging in were they not occupied by "Kung Fu" or "Batman."

Selma Fraiberg gives a sensible reason for rejecting a direct connection between normal children's viewing of violent programs and an epidemic of violence:

> I do not mean . . . that the vulgar fiction of television is capable of turning our children into delinquents. The influence of such fiction on children's attitudes and conduct is really more subtle. We need to remember that it is the parents who are the progenitors of conscience and that a child who has strong ties to his parents will not overthrow their teachings more easily than he could abandon his parents themselves. I do not think that any of us here needs to fear this kind of corruption of our children.[2]

A further flaw in the argument that violence on television might cause children to behave more violently has been stated by a television critic who points out that if this were true, there would be a concomitant effect produced by the inevitable moralistic and "good" aspects of those same violent programs:

> If indeed the cumulative watching is turning us all, gradually, into depraved beings, then the cumulative watching of good must be turning us all, gradually, into saints! You cannot have one without the other. That is, unless you are prepared to demonstrate that evil is something like cholesterol—something that slowly accumulates and clogs the system, while good is something like spinach, easily digested and quickly excreted.[3]

But if it is not the violent content of television programs that leads to violent behavior, is it merely a coincidence that the entry of television into the American home brought in its wake one of the worst epidemics of juvenile violence in the nation's history? As a professor of law and sociology stated in response to the suggestion that television is a contributing factor to juvenile violence: "I'm not suggesting a direct connection [with television] but it's inconceivable that there is no effect.[4]

There are indeed reasons to believe that television is deeply implicated in the new upsurge of juvenile aggression, particularly in the development of a new and frightening breed of juvenile offender, but those searching for a direct link between violent programs and violent actions are on a wrong tack. The *experience* of television itself (regardless of content) and its effects upon a child's perception of reality may be a more profitable line of inquiry.

Why So Much Violence?

In trying to understand the relationship between television viewing and violent behavior, one must first confront the curious fact that television today is dominated by violent programs. This was not always the case. It is noteworthy that between 1951 and 1953 there was a 15 percent increase in violent incidents on the television screen. And between 1954 and 1961 the percentage of prime-time programming devoted to action adventures featuring violence went from an average of 17 percent to about 60 percent of all programs. By 1964, according to the National Association for Better Radio and Television, almost 200 hours a week were devoted to crime scenes, with over 500 killings committed on the home screen! This reflects a 20 percent increase of violence on television over 1958 programming, and a 90 percent increase since 1952.[5]

Why did television, relatively nonviolent at its start, gradually become the hotbed of crime and mayhem it now is? Are people more fond of violence today than they were in 1950?

The answer to the first question is simple: people *want* violence on television. The rating system that effectively controls what appears on national television indicates that the public regularly chooses violent programs over more peaceful alternatives. Clearly there exists no evil conspiracy of wicked advertisers and network executives to destroy American morals and values by feeding citizens a steady diet of death and destruction. To the contrary, the advertisers meekly protest they would gladly give the public "Pollyanna" round the clock if that's what people would watch. But the rating system shows that people won't watch "Pollyanna" when they can watch "Dragnet." Advertisers want to make sure that the greatest number of people will watch *their* program, and they have learned that their chances are better if their program is action-packed.

The answer to *why* people choose to view violence on television, and why there has been an increase in violent programming in spite of periodic outcries from government investigating commissions, educators, and parents' coalitions, lies, as do all the answers to basic questions about television viewing, in the very nature of the television experience—in its essential passivity.

In viewing television the grown-up, as well as the child, is taking advantage of an easily available opportunity to withdraw from the world of activity into the realm of nondoing, nonthinking, indeed, temporary nonexisting. But the viewer does not choose to watch soothing, relaxing programs on his television set, though his main purpose in watching is often to be soothed and relaxed. Instead he opts for frantic programs filled with the most violent activities imaginable —deaths, tortures, car crashes, all to the accompaniment of frenzied music. The screen is a madhouse of activity as the viewer sits back in a paradoxical state of perfect repose.

By choosing the most active programs possible, the viewer is able to approximate a *feeling* of activity, with all the sensations of involvement, while enjoying the safety and security of total passivity. He is enjoying a *simulation* of activity in the hope that it will compensate for the actuality that he is involved in a passive, one-way experience.

Once the attraction of television violence is recognized as a compensation for the viewer's enforced passivity, the gradual increase of violence on television within the last two decades becomes understandable. For during that period not only did television ownership increase enormously, but people began to spend more of their time watching television. Between 1950 and 1975, for instance, television household use increased from 4 hours and 25 minutes per day to 6 hours and 8 minutes per day.[6] Apparently, as television viewing increases in proportion to more active experiences in people's lives, their need for the pseudo-satisfactions of simulated activity on their television screens increases as well. A quiet, contemplative, slow-paced program might only underscore the uncomfortable fact that they are not really having any experiences at all while they are watching television.

Reality and Unreality

The idea that television experiences can lead to a feeling of activity, that a person can somehow be deceived into feeling that he is *actually experiencing* those television happenings, raises a most important question about the television experience: what effect does the constant intake of simulated reality have upon the viewer's perceptions of actual reality?

Two professors at the Annenberg School of Communications at the University of Pennsylvania, Larry Gross and George Gerbner, have studied some of the effects of television "reality" upon people's ideas and beliefs pertaining to the real world. The results of their investigations suggest that the television experience impinges significantly upon viewers' perceptions of reality.

Gerbner and Gross asked heavy television viewers and light television viewers certain questions about the real world. The multiple-choice quiz offered accurate answers together with answers that reflected a bias characteristic of the television world. The researchers discovered that heavy viewers of television chose the television-biased answers far more often than they chose the accurate answers, while light viewers were more likely to choose the correct answers.

For example, the subjects were asked to guess their own chances of encountering violence in any given week. They were given the possible answers of 50–50, 10–1, and 100–1. The statistical chances that the average person will encounter personal violence in the course of a week are about 100–1, but heavy television viewers consistently chose the answers 50–50 or 10–1, reflecting the "reality" of television programs where violence prevails. The light viewers chose the right answer far more consistently.

The heavy viewers answered many other questions in a way revealing that what they saw on television had altered their perceptions of the world and society. They were more likely than light viewers to overestimate the U.S. proportion of the world population, for instance. They also overestimated the percentages of people employed as professionals, as athletes, and as entertainers in the "real world," just as television overemphasizes the importance of these groups.

Education played no significant role in ameliorating

the distortions of reality produced by heavy television watching. In most cases college-educated subjects were just as likely as those with only a grade-school education to choose the television-biased answers.[7]

The viewers' incorrect notions about the real world do not come from misleading newscasts or factual programs. The mistaken notions arise from repeated viewing of *fictional* programs performed in a realistic style within a realistic framework. These programs, it appears, begin to take on a confusing reality for the viewer, just as a very powerful dream may sometimes create confusion about whether a subsequent event was a dream or whether it actually happened. After seeing violence dealt out day after day on television programs, the viewer incorporates it into his reality, in spite of the fact that while he watches he *knows* that the programs are fictional. The violent television world distorts the viewer's perceptions of the real world, and his expectations of violence in life reflect his exposure to violence on television.

But once television fantasy becomes incorporated into the viewer's reality, the real world takes on a tinge of fantasy—or dullness because it fails to confirm the expectations created by televised "life." The separation between the real and the unreal becomes blurred; all of life becomes more dreamlike as the boundaries between the real and the unreal merge. The consequences of this merger appear in our daily papers and on the news:

People attending a real parade find it dull and say, "We should have stayed home and watched it on television. It would have been more exciting."[8]

A woman passes a burning building and says to her friend, "Don't worry, they're probably making a TV movie."[9]

Members of a real California family live out their lives in weekly installments as part of a television series, with infidelity, discovered homosexuality, and divorce happening before the viewers' very eyes, happening "for real" on TV.[10]

Thirty-seven people see a young woman murdered

in their courtyard and look on passively without coming to her aid as if it were a television drama.[11]

A seventeen-year-old boy who lived through a devastating tornado says, "Man, it was just like something on TV."[12]

Dulling Sensitivity

A disturbing possibility exists that the television experience has not merely blurred the distinctions between the real and the unreal for steady viewers, but that by doing so it has dulled their sensitivities to real events. For when the reality of a situation is diminished, people are able to react to it less emotionally, more as spectators.

An experiment devised by Dr. Victor Cline at the University of Utah Laboratories compared the emotional responses of two groups of boys between the ages of 5 and 14 to a graphically violent television program.[13] One group had seen little or no television in the previous two years. The other group had watched a great deal of television, an average of 42 hours a week for at least two years.

As the two groups of boys watched an eight-minute sequence from the Kirk Douglas movie about boxing, *Champion,* their emotional responses were recorded on a physiograph, an instrument not unlike an elaborate lie detector that measures heart action, respiration, perspiration, and other body responses.

According to their reactions as measured on the physiograph, the boys with a history of heavy television viewing were significantly less aroused by what they saw. They had, the researchers concluded, become so habituated to emotion-arousing events on television that their sensitivities had become blunted. Since they had inevitably watched many violent television programs in the course of their 42 hours of viewing a week, the researchers assumed their desensitization was an effect of constant exposure to violent content. The brunt of the author's subsequent writings has been against violence on television. In an article entitled

"Television Violence: How It Damages Your Children," Cline concludes his warnings about the dangers of television violence with a plea for better programming, and even includes a few words of praise for programs like "The Waltons."[14]

And yet the children upon whose diminished emotional reactions he based his conclusions watched 42 hours of television a week or more, while the children whose reactions were undulled watched almost no television at all. Common sense suggests that 42 hours a week of *any* television program might tip the balance from reality to unreality in a child's life sufficiently to lower his arousal level. Six hours daily of "The Waltons" seems just as likely to affect a child's ability to respond normally to human realities as an equal amount of "Mod Squad" or "Adam-12" or any of the other programs that Cline and others are exercised about.

A New Kind of Criminal

Dr. Cline's experiment requires a sensitive instrument to measure the emotional responses, or lack of them, in his young subjects. The effects of television viewing upon normal children's perceptions of and responses to real-life situations are surely subtle and measurable only with a finely calibrated machine, if at all. A different situation obtains with disturbed children, or children from pathological backgrounds. Watching television may affect such children far more profoundly.

A child therapist notes:

"I find that watching television is most destructive for psychotic children. The very thing I want to help them to understand is the real world, to increase their awareness of reality, of cause and effect. This is very much shattered by the illogic of cartoon characters being able to fly through the air, for instance, or the other fantastic things that seem so real on television. Some of these children have omnipotent fantasies. They think they can fly, too. They see someone going *zap* with his hand and making another person disappear and their omnipotent fantasy is only reinforced. Of course, the concept of one person making another disappear is also terrifying to a psychotic child, because that's what he deeply believes anyhow."

The observation that television distorts reality far more for a disturbed child than for a normal child may bear a relation to the epidemic of juvenile crime in the last two decades. For there is no doubt that the children involved in serious crimes today are not normal. Their histories reveal without exception a background of poverty, degradation, neglect, scholastic failure, frustration, family pathology . . . and heavy television viewing. But while poverty and family pathology did not appear for the first time in American society in the decades between 1952 and 1972, a frightening new breed of juvenile offender did. "It is as though our society had bred a new genetic strain," writes a reporter in *The New York Times,* "the child-murderer who feels no remorse and is scarcely conscious of his acts."[15]

Almost daily the newspapers report juvenile crimes that fill the hearts of normal readers with horror and disbelief: ten- and twelve-year-old muggers preying on the elderly, casually torturing and murdering their helpless victims, often for small gains; youths assailing a bicyclist in the park and beating him to death with a chain before escaping with his bike; kids breaking into an apartment and stomping an elderly man or drowning a woman in her bathtub.[16]

Law officers and authorities frequently blame lenient laws for the incidence of these crimes. Since in most states lawbreakers under the age of 16 are handled by a family court whose guiding philosophy is rehabilitation rather than punishment or detention for the protection of society, these young criminals need not be deterred by the fear of severe punishment: the harshest action facing a youth under 16 who commits murder in many states is confinement for up to 18 months in a public or private institution. But there is something new about these children, something that cannot be explained away as an arrogant belief that the law will be lenient toward them, that they can literally get away with murder.

"The law says a child should be treated differently, because he can be rehabilitated," says a Brooklyn police officer, "but kids weren't committing the types of crimes you see now . . . kids have changed."[17]

The common factor characterizing these "changed" kids who kill, torture, and rape seems to be a form of emotional detachment that allows them to commit unspeakable crimes with a complete absence of normal feelings such as guilt or remorse. It is as if they were dealing with inanimate objects, not with human beings at all. "It's almost as though they looked at the person who got killed as a window they were going to jimmie, as an obstacle, something that got in their way," says Charles King, director in charge of rehabilitation of New York State's Division for Youth.[18]

Today certain courts are even beginning to place juveniles in secure facilities in response to "the new type of child who is coming into the system." A psychiatrist connected with the Brooklyn Family Court describes these children as showing "a total lack of guilt and lack of respect for life. To them another person is a thing—they are wild organisms who cannot allow anyone to stand in their way."[19]

If, indeed, a new breed of juvenile offender has appeared in the last two decades, can this be accounted for by the great new element that has been introduced into children's lives within that time span—television? Poverty, family pathology, leading to severe personality disorders, neglect, inadequate schools, all these, alas, are old and familiar afflictions for certain portions of American society.

But the five, six, seven hours a day that troubled children spend watching television, more hours than they spend at any other real-life activity, is a distinctly new phenomenon. Is it possible that all these hours disturbed children spend involved in an experience that dulls the boundaries between the real and the unreal, that projects human images and the *illusion* of human feelings, while requiring no human responses from the viewer, encourages them to detach themselves from their antisocial acts in a new and horrible way?

If it is, then the total banishment of violence from the television screen will not mitigate the dehumanizing effects of long periods of television viewing upon emotionally disturbed children. For the problem is not that they learn *how* to commit violence from watching violence on television (although perhaps they sometimes do), but that television conditions them to deal with real people as if they were on a television screen. Thus they are able to "turn them off," quite simply, with a knife or a gun or a chain, with as little remorse as if they were turning off a television set.

7

Television and Play

Less Play

"Suppose there wasn't any TV—what do you think your child would do with the time now spent watching TV?"

This was one of the questions addressed to a large number of mothers of first graders in a survey published in the 1972 Surgeon General's *Report on Television and Social Behavior*. Not unexpectedly, 90 percent of the mothers answered that their child would be *playing* in some form or another if he were not watching television.[1]

It hardly requires a team of social scientists to demonstrate that television viewing keeps children from playing, for play is the major occupation of childhood. Any new activity that takes up a third or more of children's waking hours is bound to make considerable inroads into their play time.

It has been suggested that television viewing simply takes the place of other "functionally similar" activities, such as reading.[2] But that television viewing reduces play far more than reading is confirmed by an experiment in which researchers divided children into categories according to their relative use of television and books. They discovered that children who watch little television but read many books reported a higher level of daily play than either children who watched much television and read few books, or those who were heavy users of television *and* avid readers.[3] The obvious implication is that reading does not reduce children's play time significantly, while television viewing does.

The issue is simpler with preschool children: virtually all the activities young children normally engage in during their waking hours (except television viewing) fall into the category of play. When a three-year-old child builds a block castle with another child, this activity is generally regarded as play. When he pulls all the books out of his parents' bookcase, or persists in unbuttoning his shirt again and again, or tags along behind his mother pretending to sweep the floor, or picks up the phone and has a make-believe conversation, or scribbles all over the wall, or hides with his teddy bear under the bed—he is still playing. Clearly the two- or three- or four-year-old who spends two or three or four hours daily watching television is spending significantly less time playing than he would if he did not watch television at all.

Not only does television viewing lead to a reduction in play time; there is evidence to suggest that it has affected the very nature of children's play, particularly indoor play at home or in school.

An Experiment of Nature

The ideal way to discover the effects of television viewing upon young children's play would be to compare the behavior of a large, carefully-selected sample of television-watching children at play with that of a matched group of non-watchers. Such an experiment cannot be performed today for a simple reason: there *are* no non-watchers available for study. Virtually all young children watch considerable amounts of television.

Nevertheless, such an experiment comparing the play of television and non-television children was once performed. The results, however, have gone unnoticed, perhaps because it was not a deliberately designed experiment but rather what might be called an "experiment of nature," one that simply happened. It took place in the nursery schools and kindergartens of America when television was first introduced as a mass medium.

Nursery schools and kindergartens are, in their way, natural laboratories for observing children's play. Over a number of years trained teachers can perceive patterns of behavior among their young students that may not be evident to parents or professionals who work with individual children rather than children in groups. It was in these "natural" laboratories that teachers were able to observe the changes that occurred in children's play patterns as a non-television population was transformed into a television-viewing one, almost within a single decade.

Teachers who bridge the gap between the pre-television generation and the television generation are still teaching in schools throughout the country. They must be among the most dedicated and experienced early childhood educators, to have stayed with the profession so long, but their number is diminishing each year. Within the next two decades this unique group of witnesses to one of the greatest technological changes in our society will have disappeared from active professional life.

Their testimony about television's effects on children's play behavior as seen in the classroom is noteworthy:

"Children do not play the way they used to," says the principal of a private elementary school in New York and former nursery school teacher with over thirty years of teaching experience. "I don't mean outdoor play particularly. Outdoors they're still vigorous. They still climb and run and use bikes and wagons. It's inside play that has changed. You don't get as much dramatic play as you used to. Children are more interested in sitting down with so-called educational materials at a very young age. They don't seem to have as much imagination, either in verbal expression or in the ways they play or in the things they make."

"There's a greater passivity about their play," says another teacher with thirty-five years of kindergarten experience. "They'll get interested in something, but then if it means that they have to *do* something themselves, they'll lose interest."

"There's been a movement from active, impulsive kids who were just very eager to get their hands on things to do, to more cautious, passive kids with attitudes of wanting to be entertained or instructed. They don't want to just go ahead and explore by themselves," says a Denver teacher with twenty-nine years of teaching experience.

"Children expect entertainment in school. And they manage pretty well when the school work's entertaining. But their attitude is: Is this going to be fun or is it going to be boring? And if it's boring, they feel, well, you just switch the channel. Only it makes it a bit difficult in school because you can't always switch the channel," says another elementary school teacher who goes back to pre-television days.

"I find I'm having to *sell* things that are great activities that I never had to sell in the past, because some kids won't stick around long enough to find out if it's going to be fun if the first moments don't catch them. So I find I have to introduce things somewhat differently. Some children simply tune out very, very quickly," says a Riverdale, New York, nursery school teacher.

"I've had to change my style of teaching greatly over the past years," reports another kindergarten teacher whose experience spans both eras. "I used to feel free to initiate a great many activities because children then were quite capable of initiating their own activities, too. Now I get the feeling that children want me to do *all* the initiating. They'll go along with the activities I initiate, and when I don't initiate anything, they'll just wait patiently until I do. It's a kind of withdrawal on the part of the kids. Now I try to encourage kids to get involved. I try to wait and be patient while the enriched environment of the classroom comes through to the child and he accepts the invitation to make his own structure rather than to accept one made for him. But it's hard sometimes—one has to be very patient. And it's tempting to simply do *all* the initiating, because the kids will always go along so cheerfully."

"Nowadays I really feel the need to encourage children to be more active," reports another teacher. "I never felt that way twenty years ago. My word, children were too active then!"

Might the testimony of these teachers merely reflect a prejudice against a new technology, or a things-were-better-in-the-old-days way of looking at the world? Probably not, because a pattern becomes evident in their reports, a pattern that does not differ from school to school or area to area. That pattern reflects known aspects of the television experience—its essential passivity and the swiftness of its gratifications for children—making it likely that these teachers are reporting real rather than fancied changes in children's play.

Younger teachers who have taught only television-bred children share none of their older colleagues' opinions about television's influence. But the children they teach, as far as they know, represent the realities of childhood. The idea that television has affected young children's play behavior seems farfetched to them—why, they themselves were brought up watching television!

Home Play

Teachers are making great efforts, as their testimony reveals, to offset the changes they have perceived in children—increased passivity, increased impatience, increased unwillingness to put up with a slow beginning in hope for later gains—and to encourage active, imaginative play at school.

But what about children's play at home? Since home is where the set lies, there is no doubt that children do less playing at home than they once did. What about the time that remains between programs?

One change related to television is the degree of parents' involvement in their children's imaginative play. Before television it was greatly to the parent's advantage to give the child a bit of help in his play, to "start him off," as it were. The parent might initiate a make-believe game, suggest a doll tea party, for instance, or help the child get started in some other time-consuming game he would continue on his own. This practice was mutually beneficial: the parent gained free time and the child, stimulated by the adult's help, was able to play more profitably by himself.

Today a parent is far more likely to turn on the television set than to take the trouble to get a child started in a play activity, especially since the child seems just as eager—perhaps more eager—to watch television.

But might not a cleverly designed television program stimulate a child's imagination and inspire a high level of imaginative play? There is reason to believe that no matter how carefully designed and well-intentioned the guidance that comes out of a television set might be, it cannot stimulate a child's imagination nearly as well as a live person.

A Yale research group set out to assess the effects of watching a television program especially designed to stimulate the imaginations of preschool children ("Mr. Rogers' Neighborhood") upon children's imaginative play.

Four groups of children were observed at play: the first group watched "Mr. Rogers" every day for two weeks; the second group watched for the same period with an adult mediating the program's imaginative content; the third group watched no television at all but spent the same amount of time with a teacher who gave them exercises and games involving make-believe play and imagination. A control group of children watched no television and received no special adult attention.

The results revealed that the children exposed to the live adult and no television viewing at all showed the greatest increase in spontaneous imagination and pretend play. Those who watched the program with the adult intermediary present showed the next greatest gains. The two groups receiving no adult attention showed little or no gains in their imaginative play.[4]

Forms of Play

Since television viewing makes the greatest inroads into children's play and has the most visible effects upon it during the formative years of early childhood, it is necessary to examine the function of play in the development of preschool children if the overall impact of television viewing is to be understood.

The "playful" nature of children's play often obscures its importance. Far from being a mere diversion or pleasant time-filler in a child's day, play involves a critical variety of behaviors that serve important purposes in the child's social, emotional, and intellectual development. Indeed the universal appearance of play throughout the animal kingdom and the growing complexity of play as one ascends the phylogenetic ladder confirms the idea that play must have some survival value for all species that engage in it. To discover what these values are, it is useful to examine play behavior more closely and distinguish the different forms of play that children universally engage in, from the earliest stages that occur even before the child is attracted by the television set, to those advanced forms that may be displaced by television viewing in the lives of today's children.

The baby's first gropings and touchings, those various mouthings and tastings and smellings that become increasingly purposeful during the first year of life, may be seen as the beginnings of play. It is a somewhat delicate semantic problem whether to call those early exploratory activities "play" since they are generally dictated by innate instincts and are accompanied by little of the *playfulness* that characterizes play in its more advanced forms. Perhaps during that "twilight zone" of the neonatal period, when the child is still developing important neurophysiological structures, his activities might best be termed "pre-play"— or even "work." But regardless of the word used, those early explorations help the child gain his first understandings of his own self in relation to his environment. By acting out his innate instincts to explore, the child begins to differentiate himself from his mother and the world at large, and begins to learn some things about what the world is like.

In addition to providing basic understandings, the child's manipulations allow him to practice the important coordination skills that he is in the process of developing. In reaching for a toy, for instance, the child is developing eye-hand coordination, a crucial survival ability.

Not merely does the infant explore by touching, tasting, or smelling, but he explores verbally as well, by babbling and making a variety of sounds. A babbling child is clearly exploring, "trying it out" as it were, making sounds in a purposeful way with an evident interest in the results as well as the process. These verbal experiments must be seen as important precursors to language acquisition.

Another form of play appearing early in childhood involves imitation. Even before his first birthday a child will imitate certain adult movements and gestures in a playful way. (The parent claps his hands and the child claps back.) These early mimicking games provide the first opportunities for a true two-way communication even before speech is acquired. By this means the child begins to progress from a state of total receptivity to a relationship in which he is able to contribute something himself. Imitative play also includes another important stage of language learning, during which the child moves on from random babbling to a deliberate imitation of the sounds produced by people around him.

A different form of play fulfilling a different function is seen when a ten-month-old baby indulges in a game of peek-a-boo with his mother. This activity does not improve the child's mastery of physical skills nor provide information about himself or his environment, as do exploratory and imitative play. Rather, in this rudimentary version of make-believe or imaginative play the child begins to use play to serve his inner needs. He has but recently made the uncomfortable discovery that his mother, that all-important provider of food, warmth, and security, is not actually a permanent part of him, but a perfidious creature who can and does on occasion leave him entirely to himself, hungry perhaps, insecure, and filled with a dread of being permanently abandoned. This painful separation is reenacted, symbolically, in the game of peek-a-boo, but without the painful consequences of a real separation. In the game the mother comes and goes, but she is still there! Thus play helps to make difficult aspects of reality more acceptable to the young child.

Surely there is a similar, adaptive function in much of the make-believe play that young children choose to engage in and delight in. For it is easily demonstrated that they do not delight in *all* symbolic games offered by adults. Let a parent take a child's favorite blanket or cuddly toy, for instance, and pretend (all in good fun) to be about to destroy it or throw it out the window. The child will not fall into this game with playful good spirits; he will invariably react with displeasure and anxiety. This particular drama does not, it appears, serve a useful purpose for the child; it does not help to reduce his anxiety or to reassure him about an unpleasant or worrisome aspect of reality. It does not make him more comfortable with himself and his lot.

In the child's later, more complex forms of imaginative play he similarly finds ways to work out difficulties and adjust the realities of his life to his inner requirements. In make-believe play the child can take on the roles of his parents and redress grievances that have caused him suffering; he can reenact painful scenes from everyday life and transform them into more satisfactory experiences. In play he can expose, and perhaps exorcise, fears that he cannot articulate in any other way.

More important, perhaps, is the opportunity imaginative play affords the child to become an active user rather than a passive recipient of experience. In real life things seem to happen to a young child, to be *done to* him, and he is well aware of his general impotence in the power hierarchy of the world as he sees it. But in the course of his make-believe play he is allowed to reverse this balance, to *control* rather than be controlled. In the course of his play the child structures a world for himself in which he has the power to act and to affect people and events. By this symbolic though temporary reversal of the power balance, the child is able to accept his position in the real world, a position that is, he is dimly aware, also temporary.

Child's play, it can be seen, is a serious business in spite of its apparent lack of "seriousness." But perhaps the most important function served by play in children's lives does not reside in the specific forms of play, but in the social circumstances that surround it. It is likely that those play experiences he engages in with other children are of the greatest importance to his development.

The very young child does not really play "with" other children, although the presence of other children may delight and stimulate him. He plays alone or engages in what is called "parallel play," that is, he pursues his own activity in the presence of others without incorporating them into his play and without being involved in theirs. But around the age of three the child begins to take part in a more truly social form of play with other children, play involving give and take and a certain amount of mutual cooperation.

Without a doubt social play exposes the child to more dangers than solitary or parallel play or play with an indulgent parent. Playing with others requires the child to suppress his own wishes and desires to a certain degree. And this, it appears, is not an ability the child is born with: self-control must be learned. For this reason social play can be excruciatingly difficult for children at the start. Not only must each child discover the need to suppress certain of his own impulses but he must also discover the difficulties that attend the varying levels of aggression normally existing among his playmates. The more aggressive child must learn to find unaggressive ways to achieve his ends, while the milder-natured child must learn to protect himself and to maintain his integrity in the face of a more forceful companion.

As children grow and the course of their play, exploratory as well as imaginative, becomes increasingly social, their ability to control their own behavior and to influence the actions of others becomes increasingly important to their success as social creatures. While aspects of play continue to fulfill many of the same functions they once served—physical skill-developing as well as psychological-tension-relieving functions—now the acquisition of social skills and impulse control becomes the critical factor in children's play. Losing gracefully, learning to give in, getting along peacefully with others, all these are skills that children develop as they learn to play successfully with other children. The survival value of such skills in human adult life is obvious, although international wars and intrasocietal violence attest to man's imperfect attainment of them.

Play Deprivation

Since play is clearly a vehicle for many of the child's most important learnings and the means whereby he is able to practice and develop behaviors necessary to his success as a social being, what are the consequences of the loss of play time in today's children?

A famous experiment by psychologist Harry Harlow undertook to assess the general function of play in the development of a species of monkey whose play behavior exhibits many similarities to the play of human children. The findings that emerged from this and similar studies of play deprivation carry implications about the possible effects of play deprivation upon individuals of species in which playing is a normal activity—humans in particular.

Harlow observed that monkeys raised by their mothers in a normal fashion and offered normal play opportunities follow a certain pattern of behavior. During the first months of life a monkey clings tenaciously and exclusively to his mother. His first play experiences involve a variety of manipulations from the cozy safety of his mother's back. In his second or third month he begins to make sorties away from his mother in order to play with other baby monkeys. His mother aids him in his burgeoning independence, encouraging him to stop clinging and to play by pushing him away more and more often. By four months of age the young monkey spends much of his waking time in a variety of rough-and-tumble games with other monkeys, including wrestling and a kind of "tag" game.

Then Harlow observed a group of monkeys brought up normally in every respect but one: they were denied all opportunities to play with other monkeys. After eight months of play deprivation, when these monkeys were exposed to normally-reared monkeys of their own age, Harlow discovered a singular behavior anomaly in their new social relations: the play-deprived monkeys proved to be significantly *more aggressive* in their social behavior than monkeys brought up with adequate play opportunities. Though they ignored the efforts of the normal monkeys to bring them into normal play activities and withdrew from most of the rough games that characterize normal monkey play, the play-deprived monkeys initiated biting attacks on other monkeys at inappropriate times. They showed no fear of other monkeys and displayed very little control of their aggressive instincts.

It was not a matter of an increase in aggressive *instincts* among the play-deprived monkeys, for all normal monkeys manifest aggressive impulses from an early age. But the monkeys who had enjoyed regular opportunities to play from an early age clearly had learned to mitigate those aggressive instincts in the course of their daily play; little actual violence was ever inflicted by one monkey on another among the normally-reared group. In contrast, the play-deprived monkeys allowed their aggressive impulses to emerge unchecked, with unfortunate consequences for others and especially for themselves, since they often attacked monkeys much stronger than they.[5]

Harlow's studies raise a new question about the relationship between television viewing and childhood aggression: Could it be that a sizable reduction in children's play time resulting from the replacement of play activities by television viewing contributes to an increase in aggressive behavior, behavior that might once have been mitigated and socialized through play experiences?

Reduced play opportunities may indeed be responsible, to some extent, for the increase in *normal* childish aggression—pushing, shoving, hitting, and the like—that so many parents and teachers find a distressing characteristic of children's behavior today. However, it must not be construed as the single explanation for the epidemic of juvenile delinquency that has struck our society in the last two decades. Harlow's monkeys, it was noted, were brought up normally in all other respects except the elimination of play. In other experiments in which monkeys were deprived of other basic needs, maternal care, for example, far more devastating developmental changes were seen. Just so, the young people involved in real delinquency, as opposed to normal childish misbehavior, have backgrounds with far greater deprivations than play deprivation.

For normal children from normal families a lack of impulse control may not be the most significant consequence of a childhood deprived of normal play opportunities. For above all, the play of young children establishes behavior patterns that lead to a deeply satisfying way of life.

Anthropologist Edward Norbeck has written: "The primary purpose of play has a deeper importance for every individual. Playing children are motivated primarily to enjoy living. This is the major rehearsal value of play and games, for without the ability to enjoy life, the long years of adulthood can be dull and wearisome."[6]

There are indeed signs among the generation that grew up watching television that adult life *does* seem dull and wearisome, that something is missing in their enjoyment of life, something, perhaps, that a childhood of normal play might have provided.

"Many Rebels of the 1960's Depressed as They Near 30" reads a headline in *The New York Times*.[7] The article describes young people who matured during the late sixties, who are now experiencing "a generational malaise of haunting frustrations, anxiety and depression," a malaise reflected in the increase of people in their twenties and early thirties receiving psychiatric help, the rise in suicides and alcoholism in this age group, and other manifestations of an inability to "enjoy life." "I've got a good job, I'm successful, and I want to kill myself. Life doesn't mean anything," says a young person quoted in the article.

It cannot be a coincidence that the young people suffering this strange new malaise represent the first television generation. And it cannot be insignificant that they represent the first generation whose normal play activities were curtailed (in some cases virtually eliminated) as a result of involvement with television. "Pity the monkeys who are not permitted to play," writes Harry Harlow in a discussion of his experimental work. What about the children who have spent their childhood *watching* instead of playing?

8

The Television Generation

The Generation Puzzle

How does a generation acquire those particular shared patterns of behavior that characterize it and distinguish it from other generations?

"It seems inevitable," writes René Dubos, "that all changes in ways of life . . . continuously alter the perceptual world of the developing organism. New behavioral patterns and new problems of social adaptation inevitably result from such environmental changes; these, in turn, impart to individuality some characteristics that are shared by most members of a particular generation."[1]

One must discover those particular environmental changes in order to understand the etiology of a particular generation. But a puzzle remains. Babies, after all, are born every minute of every day. Does a new generation begin, then, every day? Where does one generation begin, and another end? Though environmental changes undoubtedly affect the outcome of each developing organism, if these changes are occurring continuously, as Dubos suggests, how does it happen that a particular generation will emerge differing sharply from the generation that preceded it?

To sort out the generation puzzle one must begin with two basic assumptions: first, that a generation may be defined by those great events that occur during certain periods, events that specifically alter ways of life; and second, that when such events occur, they will profoundly affect only those organisms at their most formative stages of life—that is, young children.

Thus when one talks about the Depression Generation or the World War II Generation, one does not refer to *all* people who lived through those cataclysmic and life-changing events, although indeed all people's lives were affected. One specifically means those people who were born during the years when those events occurred and whose development was likely to be affected in basic ways by the changes connected to those events.

Unlike a war or an economic disaster or a great technological advance in transportation, the coming of television did not dramatically alter people's ways of working or styles of living. It did not cause people to move in large numbers from the country to the city, or to work in factories rather than at handicrafts, or to come within easy reach and influence of people in distant parts of the world.

But one aspect of television distinguishes it from all other past technologies that have affected society. No other new development has ever affected the lives of the most vulnerable segment of the population—preschool children—as swiftly, pervasively, and *directly* as the coming of television to the American home.

The daily routine of a three-year-old was transformed by the availability of a television set to his parents. Suddenly two, three, four, even six or seven hours of his day, began to be spent at an activity that is neither sleep nor play but falls somewhere in between, an activity characterized by a novel intake of visual and auditory materials accompanied by behaviors quite uncommon among young children—silence, inactivity, mental passivity.

It is true, of course, that every new development that transforms society filters down to affect the lives of young children. If, for instance, war and its accompanying threats to life and security create an atmosphere of anxiety throughout a society, this may be assumed to affect the ways parents raise their young children and thus produce changes in an entire generation. The coming of the automobile, for example, increased mobility and so new family styles evolved. Great numbers of families abandoned established communities and severed extended-family ties to seek happiness in Suburbia—and this changed parent-child relationships and altered child development. But television touches young children's lives *directly,* more directly than any other technology or change of the past. Therefore its effects are likely to be less evolutionary in nature and more sudden in onset than those that result from other innovations.

A logical proposition suggests itself: that a child who has watched television for a quarter (or much more) of his waking hours during the critical years between two and six will be different, in important and discernible ways, from a child who has not watched television. Specifically, the television-watching child will have spent a total of at least 5,000 hours (and perhaps double that much) watching images on a screen by the time he enters the first grade. Conversely, the non-television child will have had 5,000 or more hours to devote to other formative activities during his early childhood.

If this proposition is accepted, it inevitably follows that an entity called *the television generation* exists, and that it differs from previous generations in ways related to its early television-watching experiences.

The amazing swiftness with which television was adopted makes a definable television generation easy to pinpoint. Within a narrow period of four years, between 1948 and 1952, television ownership in America rose from a few thousand to 15,000,000.[2] Thus if young children's time-consuming involvement with the television experience "imparts to individuality some characteristics that are shared by a generation," those characteristics would make their appearance more suddenly and universally than the generational changes brought about by more gradual, filtered-down effects. One might expect to see within a narrow period of time signs of television's effects upon the first generation of children to grow up with it as a formative influence.

Symptoms

Before assessing the relationship between a generation's novel behavior patterns and its television-watching experiences, it should be noted that human development is far too intricate a process for any single influence to alter the large picture in a direct and clearly defined manner. The capacities of the human body and mind to adjust to environmental stresses, those self-adjusting mechanisms that afford a constant source of second and third chances in the struggle for existence, must be taken into account.

The body has physical mechanisms, for instance, to maintain the proper inner temperature in spite of outer temperature extremes, and strategies for fighting infection and other outside invasions, and the mind has psychological means of adjusting to traumas, conflicts, and painful realities. These mechanisms by which the body and mind adjust to circumstances that threaten their equilibrium manifest themselves as *symptoms*. Shivering, coughing, vomiting, fever—all these are symptoms representing the self-repairing functions of a healthy organism, just as the neuroses, compulsions, and "irrational" behavior patterns people exhibit in the course of their lives represent psychological or emotional adjustments. An understanding of this principle forms the cornerstone of modern psychiatry, just as an understanding of the homeostatic functioning of the body underlies the practices of modern medicine.

And yet, in spite of the resilience and adaptability of the human body and mind, environmental influences *do* have lasting effects. When, for instance, one emerges in perfect health after a bout with infection, the organism has been altered in certain ways: new antibodies have been formed that will henceforth circulate in the bloodstream; certain cells have been destroyed in the battle against germs and others have been generated. Similarly the psychological adjustments a person is required to make in adapting to his life experiences leave permanent traces on his behavior even after their immediate function has been served. In plain words, people are changed by their experiences.

While certain experiences strengthen the organism, others devitalize it. Yet this is never a simple matter to assess: after a strenuous hour of weight lifting, for instance, a person is exhausted, seemingly weakened. Yet the true outcome of the exercise is a strengthening of the muscles and an increase in physical stamina. Just so, certain experiences that may seem "bad" when they occur prove, in the long run, to have invigorated rather than weakened the spirit of the one who has lived through them. A difficult job well done often leaves a residue of pleasure although the actual experience was not at all pleasant. Conversely, originally pleasurable experiences—bouts of self-indulgence, overeating, or excessive drinking—frequently leave a bad aftertaste, figuratively as well as literally, strengthening only the person's self-dissatisfaction.

What marks has a time-consuming involvement with television left on a generation of viewers? With an understanding of the nature of the television experience and the role it plays in specific areas of a young child's development, we may begin to recognize which of the behaviors that have emerged among the generation of young people first exposed to television's influence might be identified as "symptoms"—behaviors the organism has adopted to restore certain deficiencies and imbalances brought about by television's presence or, equally important, its displacement of other necessary experiences in children's lives.

Communing Without Words

Considering 1950 as the first year that television entered the American home on a large scale, then the signs of television's impact upon the first generation of children influenced by it might be expected to appear around 1964 or 1965, when those children who were 3 in 1950 approach college age. These children represent the first members of the television generation.

"The generation that came to consciousness in the 1960's is different from any generation that preceded it," writes Lawrence Fuchs.[8] But the common thread that unites and serves to define this generation is not, as Fuchs and others have suggested, a rejection of materialism and society's productivity values. Though spokesmen of this generation often dwell on their political disillusionment and other ideological conflicts to explain their alienation from society and their new life styles, their very words of explanation—stylized, inarticulate ("like, man . . . you know . . . we're just doing our thing")—and their mumbling, halting, nonsequential speaking style—as close to nonverbal speech as one can come without eliminating words entirely—indicate that a more fundamental change has occurred, one that has nothing to do with ideas or social disillusionment. The fact that the differences manifested by this generation may consistently be categorized as intensifications of nonverbal thinking patterns can hardly be unconnected with the fact that this is the first generation to have grown up watching staggering amounts of television.

A generation seems to have emerged for whom ordinary speech is not as crucial a form of communication as it has been for past generations. Direct sexual activity as a form of communication has remained unchanged—the survival of the species depends upon it. But young people going about the normal human business of establishing deep relations with each other once accomplished their ends by *talking* together, exchanging direct information. Today a circle of young people holding hands, communing with each other wordlessly, is far more characteristic than the intense coffeehouse conversations that typified the generation of the fifties. Nowadays there are new opportunities for "grooving" together in ways other than talking, for establishing intimacy by shared nonverbal experiences, often with the help of marijuana or stronger psychedelic drugs.

The Mystery of the Declining College Board Scores

The hypothesis that television viewing has affected a generation's verbal development is strengthened by the mysterious decline in the verbal aptitude scores of high school students taking the college board exams, a decline that began in 1964 and has yet to level off.[4] 1964, of course, is precisely the year that those first children exposed to large doses of television during their language-learning years sat down to take their college boards.

This simple coincidence in timing cannot be used to posit a causal relationship between television viewing and the declining scores, though it may raise suspicions that such a relationship exists. It has been suggested, for instance, that changes in teaching style or a change in the population mix of those taking the test is responsible.

But two factors help to strengthen the case for television viewing as a causative factor in the decline: the fact that the scores have *continued* to decline since 1964, and the fact that the decrease is characterized by changes in the two extremes—fewer high scores and more low scores—rather than an across-the-board slippage. Statistics of set ownership and of watching patterns illuminate these two factors.

The steady decline in scores may clearly be related to the steady increase in television ownership in the United States from 1950 on. Although television became a mass medium in 1950, only 4,000,000 television sets were sold that year. In 1955 67 percent of American households had television sets, in 1960 88 percent, in 1965 92 percent, and in 1969 95 percent of American homes had at least one set. By 1970 96 percent of the nation's families had now joined the ranks of television watchers.[5] And still the increase continued, peaking in 1975, when the Nielsen Company computed that virtually all American homes now had television.[6]

If television viewing has affected the verbal abilities

of American students, then the steady decline year after year may be explained by the steady increase in television families year after year, and the greater number of television-raised children taking the test each year. If indeed television is the culprit, then the decline should continue until around 1988, when the 1975 crop of three-year-olds reaches college board age.

Another part of the answer to the question of why the scores have declined steadily lies in the steady and considerable increase in children's viewing time since the early years of television. The average weekly television-viewing time for the 2–5 age group was 23.2 hours in 1966, 28.4 hours in 1969, and 30.41 hours in 1970. A similar increase was noted for the 6–11 age group, going from 20.9 hours of average weekly viewing time in 1966 to 25.49 hours in 1970.[7] This is a significant steady increase. Another study indicates that first and sixth graders (the two groups chosen for the study) were watching about an hour more television daily in 1970 than in 1959, and that Sunday viewing had increased by more than two and a half hours for the sixth graders.[8]

A fact which may help to explain the notable decrease in *high* scores on the college boards is that television has been making increasing inroads into the lives of *the most gifted students*. In 1959 the brightest high school students were found to be lighter viewers and heavier readers than their less gifted classmates.[9] Since in that year the situation proved to be the reverse among sixth graders (the brightest students in that grade were among the heaviest users of television), this seemed to show a promising trend, offering reassurance to anxious parents that television would have little effect on their children's destinies since by tenth grade the bright students turned to books just as they had always done.

But by 1970 this comforting trend had been reversed. The Surgeon General's report showed that now *more* of the brighter students in tenth grade were heavy users of television than heavy users of books.[10] Television now reigned supreme in the lives of the group that had once contained the most avid readers—the most gifted students.

This shift may help to explain the steady downward trend in college board scores from 1964 to this day. For as fewer gifted students sharpen their verbal abilities through reading, the likelihood that their verbal scores will go down is increased. Certainly it was this group of bright students that provided the highest scores on the college board exams. And indeed, these very scores have decreased most dramatically.

The increase in the number of low scores may reflect the influence of television as well, since it is known that television viewing increases reading difficulties.

New Patterns of Thinking and Behaving

That there is something quite different about the generation that came to maturity in the mid-sixties has been the subject of much writing and speculation. Indeed, writers have coined a variety of terms for this generation that suggest the appearance of new patterns of thinking and behaving: "Consciousness III," "the counterculture," and others. But while commentators differ about *why* these changes have occurred, it is noteworthy that their descriptions of this generation's thought and culture indicate a new preponderance of what might be called right-hemisphere ways of thinking, that is, forms of mental operation that fall under the aegis of the nonverbal, right hemisphere of the brain.

"Consciousness III is deeply suspicious of logic, rationality, analysis and principle," writes Charles Reich in *The Greening of America,* a book examining the phenomenon of a new way of thinking among young people. "It believes that thought can be 'non-linear,' spontaneous, disconnected. It thinks rational conversation has been overdone as a means of communication between people."[11]

"They assert the primacy of non-intellective powers," writes Alvin Toffler, another influential observer of the generation under discussion. He notes that one of the salient characteristics of its members is that they "call into question all that our culture values as 'reason' and 'reality.' " Theirs is a "flight from reason," he concludes.[12]

"The change from political activism to inner-directed, self-centered exploration is typical of the young generation," writes Theodore Roszak, original coiner of the term *counterculture*. "As we move along the continuum," he notes, "we find sociology giving way to psychology, political collectives yielding to the person, conscious and articulate behavior falling away before the forces of the non-intellective deep."[13]

Nonlogical, nonlinear, disconnected thought, absence of ambition, of competitive urges, disinterest in the pursuit of merit and excellence, a concentration on the self, with a preoccupation with the state of one's inner functioning (*"consciousness* consciousness" Roszak calls it), a flight from reason, from reality, from intellectual activity—all these are characteristics of the right-hemisphere mode of mental functioning. Almost invariably, each observed change in behavior among the young generation is in the direction of noncognitive, nonactive, nonverbal thinking.*

Other features of the television generation underline this trend toward the nonverbal. Although adolescents have always found particular satisfaction in listening to music, the dependence of the television generation upon music, almost to the exclusion of all other art forms, is extraordinary. "Music is the chief medium of expression, the chief means by which inner feelings are communicated," Reich observes, noting that Consciousness III has "not yet developed a widely accepted

---

*An indication of the steady decline in logical and verbal mental functioning among the television generation may be found in the most recent findings of the National Assessment of Educational Progress, released as this book was going to press. In this study thirteen- and seventeen-year-olds showed a decline in an important subcategory of the reading test, the part dealing with the ability to draw inferences from what they read. The report defined inferential comprehension as that ability in which the reader uses "the explicit information, along with his personal experiences and thinking abilities, to make predictions, form generalizations, reach conclusions, make comparisons, form judgments and create new ideas." (*Reading in America: A Prospective on Two Assessments* [Denver, Col.: National Assessment of Educational Progress, 1976.])

poetry, literature or theater; the functions of all these have so far been assumed by music . . . the dominant means of communication in our society—words— . . . [do] not seem adequate for people of the new consciousness. Music, on the other hand, says all the things they want to say or feel."[14]

A number of scientists have demonstrated the particular role played by the right hemisphere in the mental processes associated with musical ability and musical cognition. Patients suffering complete loss of language due to left-hemisphere surgery nevertheless demonstrate an ability to sing songs, to play the piano, and to gain pleasure from listening to music. Conversely, it has been found that right-hemisphere damage causes defects in the understanding of musical sounds far more than in any verbal capacities. Thus it is understandable that a generation that received particular stimulation to right-hemisphere organizations in its formative years has an extraordinary dependence on musical experiences.

"The interest of our college-age and adolescent young in the psychology of alienation, Oriental mysticism, psychedelic drugs and communal experiments make for a cultural constellation that radically diverges from values and assumptions that have been in the mainstream of our society at least since the scientific revolution of the seventeenth century," writes Roszak.[15]

Television and Drugs

Psychedelic drugs—it is here that a disquieting image enters the picture of this brave new generation. A new trend toward feeling rather than thinking might not necessarily be for the bad. *So what* if a new right-hemisphere orientation is beginning to replace the former dominance of verbal thinking, of ambition, of goal-centered activities and behaviors, one might ask. Might this not represent an improvement in a society with a decreasingly humanistic focus, as Reich and Roszak and Toffler believe? Even the increasing involvement of this generation with the Irrational—with astrology, witchcraft, numerology, palmistry, the language of flowers, and any number of other pseudo-sciences that seem to spring up from every crack in the old rational order—might still be looked upon as a healthy antidote to the super-rational directions the technocracy has taken.

But the appearance of drugs as an important part of the television generation's culture cannot be easily accepted as a promising development. And drug use may be the "symptom" bearing the greatest relevance to this generation's television-watching experiences.

Between 1964 and 1968, precisely when the first members of the television generation began to come of age, the proportion of young people between the ages of 10 and 18 arrested as users of dangerous drugs *doubled*.[16] Certainly this does not prove that television viewing and drug use are causally related; other important factors, including the increased availability of drugs, are relevant. But the curious coincidence of timing between the two suggests a connection between the television experience and the new incidence of drug use among young people.

Young people themselves frequently associate drug use and the television experience:

"Sure I use pot. It feels good. Pot slows the world down a little. I listen to myself better. Slow and hazy, but somehow clear, like a movie in slow motion or a TV show with a screen so small it goes right into your head so you can feel what it shows on the pictures," says a nineteen-year-old quoted in a study published in 1972.

"Hell I used grass since I was fourteen," reports a seventeen-year-old. "This year I dropped acid for a while. . . . All the pictures inside my eyeballs made me think about the country and me. . . . I watched them from here like on a TV show."

The authors of the study note: "Similar references to television appear again and again in our interviews."[17]

A young writer of the television generation defends his commitment to drug experiences:

"Under its influence [marijuana] . . . you don't have to say anything to have a perception and ap-perception enhanced. Without words it's possible to assess your psychological self-structure . . . and the first thing you learn is that you can no longer make the value judgement between what is real and what is not. Just like with TV."[18]

The writer concludes an argument in favor of drug use with a revealing statement: "America will simply have to realize and sanction the notion that the wide-spread experimentation with drugs is not a symptom of decadence, but, on the contrary, one of adaptation."

It is a curious notion, that a generation's involvement with mind-altering drugs represents an adaptation to some aspect of their environment. In *Future Shock* Alvin Toffler suggests that overstimulation at the sensory level ultimately interferes with people's actual ability to think, leading to an adaptive response involving withdrawal, apathy, and a rejection of reason and rational thinking altogether. "The United States," writes Toffler, "is a nation in which tens of thousands of young people flee reality by opting for drug-induced lethargy. . . . By blindly stepping up the rate of change, the level of novelty, and the extent of choice, we are condemning millions to future shock. We are thought-lessly tampering with the environmental preconditions of rationality."[19]

Yet there is something unsatisfactory about the no-tion that such factors as an increased rate of change or a staggering variety of choices have led to so important a behavioral change among a generation of children as a widespread use of drugs. Surely the preconditions of rationality are not environmental, but lie in the mental development of the would-be rational individual. The most effective tampering, surely, would involve ex-periences during early childhood, when those basic structures of rationality are formed.

Pure Awareness

If the television experience that plays so important a role in the lives of young children today is understood to involve mental activities closer to those experienced in a drugged state than to those of normal waking consciousness, then perhaps a connection between a generation's drug involvement and its early television experiences will begin to seem possible.

Compare the waking state of consciousness, against which we measure all other states of awareness that might be considered abnormal or changed, with some common aspects of the television experience. In most of our waking moments our minds take in a variety of sensory material and proceed to transform it with thoughts. As we experience each waking moment, the mind compares, considers, weighs, checks, and invests with meaning the sensory material coming in from the outside world. That is to say, the mind interprets data even as it is perceiving it. We cannot stop thinking; it is our normal mental activity and we do it quite automatically. Indeed we are so accustomed to this mental activity that its absence makes us feel strange, "unreal."

When absorbed in a television experience, our minds take in perceptual data, but the sensations of the experience fill up the mind far more fully than the normal experiences of real life. In most normal television perception, little thinking or interpreting or remembering accompanies the viewing. The viewer is so completely absorbed in the television experience, especially the young viewer, that he can hardly manipulate the sensations as he does real-life material. The mind takes in the television images as they arrive and stores them intact.

The television-viewing state of consciousness is not far removed from that state described by drug users as *pure awareness,* in which ". . . the person is completely and vividly aware of his experience, but there are no processes of thinking, manipulating, or interpreting going on. The sensations fill the person's attention, which is passive, but absorbed in what is occurring, which is usually experienced as intense and immediate. Pure awareness is experiencing without associations to what is there."[20]

The conscious awareness that characterizes our normal way of perceiving connects our sensory experiences to meanings, plans, and possible actions. But in the state of pure awareness common to many drug experiences "objects are experienced as sensory qualities, without the intrusion of interpretation."[21]

Of course there are times when we bring all our intellectual faculties into play when watching television. Certainly variations in viewing style are possible, and they depend, at least in part, upon the content and artistic value of the program. So a viewer *may* utilize his normal style of mental attention when watching television. But this does not seem to be the *usual* viewing style, as evidenced by the universal use of television as a relaxing, "unwinding," sedating agent. Normal, conscious awareness requires a certain alertness and tension that are antithetical to relaxation. It is far more likely that normal, everyday television viewing involves a different state of consciousness than that of normal waking life.

A typical description of a drug-like use of television:

"I come home and I'm exhausted, too tired to read or really *do* anything. So I just turn on the television and it mesmerizes me. I use it as a tranquilizer," says a young nursery school teacher.

A working mother says:

"I have a television because I need sometimes to be totally fed by this box. I don't have to do a thing, I can just completely relax. It takes care of me. I don't have to respond. I don't have to give anything to it."

The Drug Epidemic

If indeed there is something similar about the state of mind during the television experience and during a drug experience, then the argument that there is a relationship between the sudden emergence of drug use by young people in the mid-1960s and the fact that those same young people were the first to grow up watching great amounts of television is strengthened.

For it does not seem unreasonable to suggest that a time-consuming involvement, almost an indoctrination, into a particular style of consciousness different from the normal one would leave a generation predisposed to other experiences that restore them to a similar mental condition.

But in considering the influence of the television experience upon the generation of the sixties and in trying to understand its connection with their large-scale use of drugs, a purely neurophysiological approach (right-hemisphere stimulation over left) or any other single explanation is insufficient. Other important psychological and sociological factors are implicated in the drug epidemic that hit the cities, suburbs, campuses, and school yards of America in the mid-sixties, but invariably they are relevant only when combined with the television factor.

A number of explanations have been offered by a variety of experts for the drug explosion in the mid-sixties. Although these explanations seem reasonable, even likely, they do not answer the crucial question— *why precisely then?* Only when television is added as the new ingredient that entered children's lives around 1950 do any of the accepted hypotheses for why young people resort to drugs seem reasonable.

Here are some of the explanations that have been offered by writers and social scientists for the use of drugs by young people in the 1960s:

"The thirst for experience moves the young towards whatever promises knowledge, drama, or merely more. . ."[22]

"The pressures upon them are internal: an inner vacancy in the midst of plenty. They seek release from *what they have not got:* a way out of a constricting world bled of color and life."[23]

"The alienation of the young is not a passing phase nor a childhood disease. It is an almost total isolation of the ego without connection to others or the soul: a profound cultural anomie expressed as a distressed yearning not only for comrades but for emotions locked within the self. . . ."[24]

"What the young want . . . is that the prize be located at the top of the Crackerjack box, not at the bottom. The attraction of drugs . . . is precisely that they allow the illusion of intense and immediate experience that is almost totally and safely referential to the self and not the world. Unfortunately, the sense of self remains pathetically thin. . . . It is not that they 'drop out' but that they have not as yet been 'turned on' by the world. Even with the drug experience they continue to ask: 'What is there to do?' It is not that they are frantic or full of inner turmoil, but that they are bored."[25]

In each case television provides the answer to the question of *why just then:*

The "thirst for experience" that appeared in the mid-sixties may well reflect a childhood spent in a desert of real-life experiences, since the ordinary sensory experiments of childhood were diminished by a time-consuming engagement with television.

A "world bled of color and life" almost perfectly describes the television world. What better explanation for a feeling of "inner vacancy" than a childhood spent watching television?

Why shouldn't a child who has spent more time watching television than talking to parents, playing with friends, or forming human relationships not reach the threshold of adulthood with strong feelings of cultural "anomie" and isolation?

Isn't it likely that a child brought up with a television set ever available to alleviate emptiness and boredom would show an "increased intolerance for anxiety and frustration"?

Wouldn't a childhood spent with more hours before a television set than engaged in real-life activities leave a child with "a sense of self that remains pathetically thin"?

There is no *proof* that television viewing is seriously related to declining verbal abilities, to the appearance of a new life style, to alarming trends such as drug use and drug abuse among increasing numbers of young people. But when all the elements of the puzzle are brought together and examined, television seems seriously implicated in the outcome of the first generation that grew up under its influence. And something is odd about the new generation, something is wrong, somehow. . . .

Joyce Maynard, an anomalously articulate representative of the television generation, draws a sad picture:

Oh yes, I know we are the Pepsi Generation. I know what they say about our "youthful exuberance," our music, our clothes, our freedom and energy and go-power. And it's true that physically we're strong and energetic, and that we dance and surf and ride around on motorbikes and stay up all night while the parents shake their heads and say "Oh, to be young again. . . ." What sticks in my head, though, is another image. I hear low, barely audible speech, words breathed out as if by some supreme and nearly superhuman effort. I see limp gestures and sedentary figures. Kids sitting listening to music, sitting rapping, just sitting. We're tired, often more from boredom than exertion, old without being wise, worldly not from seeing the world but from watching it on television.[26]

III

TELEVISION AND THE FAMILY

9

Family Life

A quarter of a century after the introduction of television into American society, a period that has seen the medium become so deeply ingrained in American life that in at least one state the television set has attained the rank of a legal necessity, safe from repossession in case of debt along with clothes, cooking utensils, and the like,[1] television viewing has become an inevitable and ordinary part of daily life. Only in the early years of television did writers and commentators have sufficient perspective to separate the activity of watching television from the actual content it offers the viewer. In those early days writers frequently discussed the effects of television on family life. However, a curious myopia afflicted those early observers: almost without exception they regarded television as a favorable, beneficial, indeed, wondrous influence upon the family.

"Television is going to be a real asset in every home where there are children," predicts a writer in 1949.[2]

"Television will take over your way of living and change your children's habits, but this change can be a wonderful improvement," claims another commentator.[3]

"No survey's needed, of course, to establish that television has brought the family together in one room," writes *The New York Times* television critic in 1949.[4]

Each of the early articles about television is invariably accompanied by a photograph or illustration showing a family cozily sitting together before the television set, Sis on Mom's lap, Buddy perched on the arm of Dad's chair, Dad with his arm around Mom's shoulder. Who could have guessed that twenty or so years later Mom would be watching a drama in the kitchen, the kids would be looking at cartoons in their room, while Dad would be taking in the ball game in the living room?

Of course television sets were enormously expensive in those early days. The idea that by 1975 more than 60 percent of American families would own two or more sets was preposterous. The splintering of the multiple-set family was something the early writers could not foresee. Nor did anyone imagine the number of hours children would eventually devote to television, the common use of television by parents as a child pacifier, the changes television would effect upon child-rearing methods, the increasing domination of family schedules by children's viewing requirements —in short, the *power* of the new medium to dominate family life.

After the first years, as children's consumption of the new medium increased, together with parental concern about the possible effects of so much television viewing, a steady refrain helped to soothe and reassure anxious parents. "Television always enters a pattern of influences that already exist: the home, the peer group, the school, the church and culture generally," write the authors of an early and influential study of television's effects on children.[5] In other words, if the child's home life is all right, parents need not worry about the effects of all that television watching.

But television does not merely influence the child; it deeply influences that "pattern of influences" that is meant to ameliorate its effects. Home and family life have changed in important ways since the advent of television. The peer group has become television-oriented, and much of the time children spend together is occupied by television viewing. Culture generally has been transformed by television. Therefore it is improper to assign to television the subsidiary role its many apologists (too often members of the television industry) insist it plays. Television is not merely one of a number of important influences upon today's child.

Through the changes it has made in family life, television emerges as *the* important influence in children's lives today.

The Quality of Family Life

Television's contribution to family life has been an equivocal one. For while it has, indeed, kept the members of the family from dispersing, it has not served to bring them *together*. By its domination of the time families spend together, it destroys the special quality that distinguishes one family from another, a quality that depends to a great extent on what a family *does*, what special rituals, games, recurrent jokes, familiar songs, and shared activities it accumulates.

"Like the sorcerer of old," writes Uric Bronfenbrenner, "the television set casts its magic spell, freezing speech and action, turning the living into silent statues so long as the enchantment lasts. The primary danger of the television screen lies not so much in the behavior it produces—although there is danger there—as in the behavior it prevents: the talks, the games, the family festivities and arguments through which much of the child's learning takes place and through which his character is formed. Turning on the television set can turn off the process that transforms children into people."[6]

Yet parents have accepted a television-dominated family life so completely that they cannot see how the medium is involved in whatever problems they might be having. A first-grade teacher reports:

"I have one child in the group who's an only child. I wanted to find out more about her family life because this little girl was quite isolated from the group, didn't make friends, so I talked to her mother. Well, they don't have time to do anything in the evening, the mother said. The parents come home after picking up the child at the baby-sitter's. Then the mother fixes dinner while the child watches TV. Then they have dinner and the child goes to bed. I said to this mother, 'Well, couldn't she help you fix dinner? That would be a nice time for the two of you to talk,' and the mother said, 'Oh, but I'd hate to have her miss "Zoom." It's such a good program!' "

Even when families make efforts to control television, too often its very presence counterbalances the positive features of family life. A writer and mother of two boys aged 3 and 7 described her family's television schedule in an article in *The New York Times:*

> We were in the midst of a full-scale War. Every day was a new battle and every program was a major skirmish. We agreed it was a bad scene all around and were ready to enter diplomatic negotiations. . . . In principle we have agreed on 2½ hours of TV a day, "Sesame Street," "Electric Company" (with dinner gobbled up in between) and two half-hour shows between 7 and 8:30 which enables the grown-ups to eat in peace and prevents the two boys from destroying one another. Their pre-bedtime choice is dreadful, because, as Josh recently admitted, "There's nothing much on I really like." So . . . it's "What's My Line" or "To Tell the Truth." . . . Clearly there is a need for first-rate children's shows at this time. . . .[7]

Consider the "family life" described here: Presumably the father comes home from work during the "Sesame Street"—"Electric Company" stint. The children are either watching television, gobbling their dinner, or both. While the parents eat their dinner in peaceful privacy, the children watch another hour of television. Then there is only a half-hour left before bedtime, just enough time for baths, getting pajamas on, brushing teeth, and so on. The children's evening is regimented with an almost military precision. They watch their favorite programs, and when there is "nothing much on I really like," they watch whatever else is on—because *watching* is the important thing. Their mother does not see anything amiss with watching programs just for the sake of watching; she only wishes there were some first-rate children's shows on at those times.

Without conjuring up memories of the Victorian era with family games and long, leisurely meals, and large families, the question arises: isn't there a better family life available than this dismal, mechanized arrangement of children watching television for however long is allowed them, evening after evening?

Of course, families today still do *special* things together at times: go camping in the summer, go to the zoo on a nice Sunday, take various trips and expeditions. But their *ordinary* daily life together is diminished—that sitting around at the dinner table, that spontaneous taking up of an activity, those little games invented by children on the spur of the moment when there is nothing else to do, the scribbling, the chatting, and even the quarreling, all the things that form the fabric of a family, that define a childhood. Instead, the children have their regular schedule of television programs and bedtime, and the parents have their peaceful dinner together.

The author of the article in the *Times* notes that "keeping a family sane means mediating between the needs of both children and adults."[8] But surely the needs of adults are being better met than the needs of the children, who are effectively shunted away and rendered untroublesome, while their parents enjoy a life as undemanding as that of any childless couple. In reality, it is those very demands that young children make upon a family that lead to growth, and it is the way parents accede to those demands that builds the relationships upon which the future of the family depends. If the family does not accumulate its backlog of shared experiences, shared *everyday* experiences that occur and recur and change and develop, then it is not likely to survive as anything other than a caretaking institution.

Family Rituals

Ritual is defined by sociologists as "that part of family life that the family likes about itself, is proud of and wants formally to continue."[9] Another text notes that "the development of a ritual by a family is an index of the common interest of its members in the family as a group."[10]

What has happened to family rituals, those regular, dependable, recurrent happenings that gave members of a family a feeling of *belonging* to a home rather than living in it merely for the sake of convenience, those experiences that act as the adhesive of family unity far more than any material advantages?

Mealtime rituals, going-to-bed rituals, illness rituals, holiday rituals, how many of these have survived the inroads of the television set?

A young woman who grew up near Chicago reminisces about her childhood and gives an idea of the effects of television upon family rituals:

"As a child I had millions of relatives around—my parents both come from relatively large families. My father had nine brothers and sisters. And so every holiday there was this great swoop-down of aunts, uncles, and millions of cousins. I just remember how wonderful it used to be. These thousands of cousins would come and everyone would play and ultimately, after dinner, all the women would be in the front of the house, drinking coffee and talking, all the men would be in the back of the house, drinking and smoking, and all the kids would be all over the place, playing hide and seek. Christmas time was particularly nice because everyone always brought all their toys and games. Our house had a couple of rooms with go-through closets, so there were always kids running in a great circle route. I remember it was just wonderful.

"And then all of a sudden one year I remember becoming suddenly aware of how different everything had become. The kids were no longer playing Monopoly or Clue or the other games we used to play together. It was because we had a television set which had been turned on for a football game. All of that socializing that had gone on previously had ended. Now everyone was sitting in front of the television set, on a holiday, at a family party! I remember being stunned by how awful that was. Somehow the television had become more attractive."

As families have come to spend more and more of their time together engaged in the single activity of television watching, those rituals and pastimes that once gave family life its special quality have become more and more uncommon. Not since prehistoric times when cave families hunted, gathered, ate, and slept, with little time remaining to accumulate a culture of any significance, have families been reduced to such a sameness.

Real People

It is not only the activities that a family might engage in together that are diminished by the powerful presence of television in the home. The relationships of the family members to each other are also affected, in both obvious and subtle ways. The hours that the young child spends in a one-way relationship with television people, an involvement that allows for no communication or interaction, surely affect his relationships with real-life people.

Studies show the importance of eye-to eye contact, for instance, in real-life relationships, and indicate that the nature of a person's eye-contact patterns, whether he looks another squarely in the eye or looks to the side or shifts his gaze from side to side, may play a significant role in his success or failure in human relationships.[11] But no eye contact is possible in the child-television relationship, although in certain children's programs people purport to speak directly to the child and the camera fosters this illusion by focusing directly upon the person being filmed. (Mr. Rogers is an example, telling the child "I like you, you're special," etc.). How might such a distortion of real-life relationships affect a child's development of trust, of openness, of an ability to relate well to other *real* people?

Bruno Bettelheim writes:

Children who have been taught, or conditioned, to listen passively most of the day to the warm verbal communications coming from the TV screen, to the deep emotional appeal of the so-called TV personality, are often unable to respond to real persons because they arouse so much less feeling than the skilled actor. Worse, they lose the ability to learn from reality because life experiences are much more complicated than the ones they see on the screen. . . .[12]

A teacher makes a similar observation about her personal viewing experiences:

"I have trouble mobilizing myself and dealing with real people after watching a few hours of television. It's just hard to make that transition from watching television to a real relationship. I suppose it's because there was no effort necessary while I was watching, and dealing with real people always requires a bit of effort. Imagine, then, how much harder it might be to do the same thing for a small child, particularly one who watches a lot of television every day."

But more obviously damaging to family relationships is the elimination of opportunities to talk, and perhaps more important, to argue, to air grievances, between parents and children and brothers and sisters. Families frequently use television to avoid confronting their problems, problems that will not go away if they are ignored but will only fester and become less easily resolvable as time goes on.

A mother reports:

"I find myself, with three children, wanting to turn on the TV set when they're fighting. I really have to struggle not to do it because I feel that's telling them this is the solution to the quarrel—but it's so tempting that I often do it."

A family therapist discusses the use of television as an avoidance mechanism:

"In a family I know the father comes home from work and turns on the television set. The children come and watch with him and the wife serves them their meal in front of the set. He then goes and takes a shower, or works on the car or something. She then goes and has her own dinner in front of the television set. It's a symptom of a deeper-rooted problem, sure. But it would help them all to get rid of the set. It would be far easier to work on what the symptom really means without the television. The television simply encourages a double avoidance of each other. They'd find out more quickly what was going on if they weren't able to hide behind the TV. Things wouldn't necessarily be better, of course, but they wouldn't be anesthetized."

The decreased opportunities for simple conversation between parents and children in the television-centered home may help explain an observation made by an emergency room nurse at a Boston hospital. She reports that parents just seem to sit there these days when they come in with a sick or seriously injured child, although talking to the child would distract and comfort him. "They don't seem to know *how* to talk to their own children at any length," the nurse observes. Similarly, a television critic writes in *The New York Times:* "I had just a day ago taken my son to the emergency ward of a hospital for stitches above his left eye, and the occasion seemed no more real to me than Maalot or 54th Street, south-central Los Angeles. There was distance and numbness and an inability to turn off the total institution. I didn't behave at all; I just watched. . . ."[13]

A number of research studies substantiate the assumption that television interferes with family activities and the formation of family relationships. One survey shows that 78 percent of the respondents indicate no conversation taking place during viewing except at specified times such as commercials. The study notes: "The television atmosphere in most households is one of quiet absorption on the part of family members who are present. The nature of the family social life during a program could be described as 'parallel' rather than interactive, and the set does seem to dominate family life when it is on."[14] Thirty-six percent of the respondents in another study indicated that television viewing was the only family activity participated in during the week.[15]

In a summary of research findings on television's effect on family interactions James Gabardino states: "The early findings suggest that television had a disruptive effect upon interaction and thus presumably human development. . . . It is not unreasonable to ask: 'Is the fact that the average American family during the 1950's came to include two parents, two children and a television set somehow related to the psychosocial characteristics of the young adults of the 1970's?' "[16]

Undermining the Family

In its effect on family relationships, in its facilitation of parental withdrawal from an active role in the socialization of their children, and in its replacement of family rituals and special events, television has played an important role in the disintegration of the American family. But of course it has not been the only contributing factor, perhaps not even the most important one. The steadily rising divorce rate, the increase in the number of working mothers, the decline of the extended family, the breakdown of neighborhoods and communities, the growing isolation of the nuclear family—all have seriously affected the family.

As Urie Bronfenbrenner suggests, the sources of family breakdown do not come from the family itself, but from the circumstances in which the family finds itself and the way of life imposed upon it by those circumstances. "When those circumstances and the way of life they generate undermine relationships of trust and emotional security between family members, when they make it difficult for parents to care for, educate and enjoy their children, when there is no support or recognition from the outside world for one's role as a parent and when time spent with one's family means frustration of career, personal fulfillment and peace of mind, then the development of the child is adversely affected," he writes.[17]

But while the roots of alienation go deep into the fabric of American social history, television's presence in the home fertilizes them, encourages their wild and unchecked growth. Perhaps it is true that America's commitment to the television experience masks a spiritual vacuum, an empty and barren way of life, a desert of materialism. But it is television's dominant role in the family that anesthetizes the family into accepting its unhappy state and prevents it from struggling to better its condition, to improve its relationships, and to regain some of the richness it once possessed.

Others have noted the role of mass media in perpetuating an unsatisfactory *status quo*. Leisure-time activity, writes Irving Howe, "must provide relief from work monotony without making the return to work too unbearable; it must provide amusement without insight and pleasure without disturbance—as distinct from art which gives pleasure through disturbance. Mass culture is thus oriented towards a central aspect of industrial society: the depersonalization of the individual."[18] Similarly, Jacques Ellul rejects the idea that television is a legitimate means of educating the citizen: "Education . . . takes place only incidentally. The clouding of his consciousness is paramount. . . ."[19]

And so the American family muddles on, dimly aware that something is amiss but distracted from an understanding of its plight by an endless stream of television images. As family ties grow weaker and vaguer, as children's lives become more separate from their parents', as parents' educational role in their children's lives is taken over by television and schools, family life becomes increasingly more unsatisfying for both parents and children. All that seems to be left is Love, an abstraction that family members *know* is necessary but find great difficulty giving each other because the traditional opportunities for expressing love within the family have been reduced or destroyed.

For contemporary parents, love toward each other has increasingly come to mean successful sexual relations, as witnessed by the proliferation of sex manuals and sex therapists. The opportunities for manifesting other forms of love through mutual support, understanding, nurturing, even, to use an unpopular word, *serving* each other, are less and less available as mothers and fathers seek their independent destinies outside the family.

As for love of children, this love is increasingly expressed through supplying material comforts, amusements, and educational opportunities. Parents show their love for their children by sending them to good schools and camps, by providing them with good food and good doctors, by buying them toys, books, games, and a television set of their very own. Parents will even go further and express their love by attending PTA meetings to improve their children's schools, or by joining groups that are acting to improve the quality of their children's television programs.

But this is love at a remove, and is rarely understood by children. The more direct forms of parental love require time and patience, steady, dependable, ungrudgingly given time actually spent *with* a child, reading to him, comforting him, playing, joking, and working with him. But even if a parent were eager and willing to demonstrate that sort of direct love to his children today, the opportunities are diminished. What with school and Little League and piano lessons and, of course, the inevitable television programs, a day seems to offer just enough time for a good-night kiss.

10

Parents of the Past

Bringing up a young child is not an easy matter. The child's energy, curiosity, irrationality, persistence, emotional instability, and, most of all, unpredictability—all normal characteristics of his development—often make child rearing a trying job.

Although styles in child rearing have changed from period to period in history, and attitudes toward children have undergone a virtual revolution, we can assume nevertheless that the basic needs and behaviors of children in their early years have not changed, and that during the first five years of life children of the past behaved in ways that were not very different from the ways children behave today. That is to say, they were frequently troublesome, by the very nature of their immaturity. It is mainly the behavior of parents toward children that has changed.

Television has brought the modern parent instant relief from the difficulties of child care by transforming a third or more of the preschool child's waking hours from unpredictable activity to dependable passivity. In order to gain a perspective on how and why modern parents use television to accommodate to the difficulties of living with young children, it is useful to look back at the ways parents of the past coped with similar difficulties.

Neglect and Brutality

"The history of childhood," writes psychoanalyst Lloyd de Mause, "is a nightmare from which we have only recently begun to awake."[1] That nightmare, in which neglect and brutality epitomized the ways adults dealt with young children, encompassed most of recorded history. The biblical injunction "spare the rod and spoil the child" was once followed with an awesome zeal; in past eras children were beaten regularly and savagely, sometimes to within an inch of their lives. Nor was child beating performed secretly; children were beaten publicly and deliberately, in classrooms, in family parlors, before audiences of relatives and friends, wherever and whenever the need arose.

Terrorizing children was once a common practice. Seventeenth-century parents, for example, commonly brought their small sons and daughters to witness public hangings and executions in order to frighten them into compliant behavior. And from the earliest known times children were frightened with stories of witches and monsters waiting to pounce on them if they misbehaved. Although vestiges of this practice remain today in certain folk tales and legends, the horror stories these have evolved from were once presented so graphically and dramatically that histories record incidents of young children being literally frightened to death.[2]

Starvation and food deprivation were yet other common means of controlling children's behavior (surviving only in vestigial versions such as "no dessert if you don't behave"). Moreover a wide variety of sedatives and depressants for children, labeled with names such as "The Mother's Helper" or "Mothers' Blessing," were once freely available to parents seeking relief from the normal behavior of young children. Containing enough laudanum or cocaine or opium to render a small child passive if not altogether comatose, these potions were effective in subduing the child's natural activity and eliminating the troubles such activities might cause a parent or caretaker.

Child abuse, of course, has not been eliminated today. A great number of "battered babies" and grievously mistreated children still make their way to hospital wards and public agencies and thence to the attention of the general public. And a substantial amount of violence toward young children remains hidden behind family walls. Brutal and violent treatment of children, however, is an aberration today, subject to actual criminal sanctions. Child beating or starving or terrorizing are universally held to be reprehensible coping methods, though some parents still resort to them. Yet these practices were regarded as normal and acceptable as recently as a hundred years ago.

Most parents today are prevented by conscience from inflicting physical or mental pain upon their young children. How is it, then, that parents of the past could treat their children this way without guilt or remorse? The answer is clear: nothing short of a universal change in consciousness about the nature of children and childhood could have led to a reversal in thinking so great that behavior once common and acceptable came to seem wicked and even pathological.

The crucial catalyst for this change in thinking lay in a new awareness of the special needs of the young child, needs that must be distinguished from those of parents. For without such an awareness parents were free to behave toward children in ways that emphasized their *own* needs, and to employ child-rearing methods purely because they were efficacious, with no regard for the effects they might have upon the child's development. Not until a parent came to consider the child as a creature with special needs, and not until he came to understand these needs and to separate them from his own, could he be constrained to modify his behavior toward his child so as to prevent the child's suffering.

Without this conception that there was something special and different about a child's nature and needs, the parent of the past often regarded the child's naturally "childish" behavior as a manifestation of the parent's own undesirable tendencies. In beating or terrorizing the child a parent was able to deal freely with his own hostilities, frustrations, fears, and secret desires. He felt no guilt or remorse at his brutality toward the child because the child did not really exist —he merely embodied his parent's inner needs.

An example of such parental projection may be seen in an incident from colonial American history. When the small child of the renowned American clergyman and author Cotton Mather fell into a fire and sustained serious injuries, her father cried out, "Alas, for my sins the just God throws my child into the fire!"[3] The father's belief that *he* was the sufferer in this case rather than the child, his lack of sympathy for the child's suffering (to say nothing of his lack of remorse at the negligence that allowed such an accident to occur), makes it clear that he regarded his child in an entirely different light than parents today regard their children.

A New Light on Childhood

Beginning with Rousseau's writings in the eighteenth century, new light was cast upon the special nature and needs of children. Slowly and steadily new ideas spread and filtered through all levels of society, starting with the educated classes and gradually making their way to those classes of society most resistant to change. The transformation in thinking about children culminated with the writings of Freud and his followers and with the creation of an entirely new discipline, child psychology. The era of the child as a creature of special needs had arrived. And just as today a change in consciousness about women has led to great changes in men's behavior toward women (and women's behavior toward men and each other), so the new ideas about childhood and children brought about a true revolution in child care, revolution marked by a shift in emphasis from the parent's needs to the newly recognized needs of the child. An empathetic style of child rearing was born, one that had repercussions not only in the new parental ways of dealing with children's behavior, but also in children's own ways of behaving and adapting.

Instead of using corporal punishment, food deprivation, terrorization, and other powerful behavior modifiers, parents began to turn to more "psychological" methods of discipline—reasoning, cajoling, distracting, withdrawing approval, and the like. But while these methods reflected the new understanding of child development and promoted the child's basic needs, there was a problem from the parent's point of view: these methods did not always work efficiently. Reasoning with a young child engaged in a particularly delightful infraction, after all, rarely works as effectively, and never as swiftly, as a quick whack. As a result, while young children flourished under a more humanistic child-rearing system, parents conscientiously striving to fulfill the child's developmental needs often found it far more difficult to fulfill their own adult needs.

One difficulty facing parents in the new empathetic child-rearing era stemmed from the dawning awareness that it was not necessarily "good" for a child to be good. In the old unenlightened days the emphasis in child rearing was on character development. To be good was the major expectation for a child. Since a "good" child is an untroublesome one, and since being good requires the child to behave in ways that do not conflict with adult needs, this criterion may be seen at once as a manifestation of a child-rearing methodology constructed around parents' needs.

In the new era parents were obliged to cope with behaviors that seriously interfered with their adult lives, with those normal gropings and grabbings, throwings, interruptings, vocalizings, and demandings—behaviors that were once considered "bad" and punished out of existence—in new ways that required more time and effort. As the ideal of "goodness" and character development was replaced by the new *summum bonum* of emotional security the parent's lot became harder. And the difficulty was further increased by a new awareness that those very years when children make the most demands on parents' time and energies, when they are the most difficult to handle—the years, that is, of early childhood—are of critical importance to the child's acquisition of that much desired emotional security. Not only did parents now have to be more tolerant of child behavior that interfered with their adult life, but they also felt a compulsion to spend *more* time with their children, correctly believing that this helped build the crucial foundations for the child's emotional and intellectual future.

Moreover, in the new era of child care, not merely were parents restrained by their own empathetic feelings from employing brutality, but they also found themselves unable to operate in the casual and neglectful style that had made the job of a parent so much simpler in the past. It may appear that the greater work burdens of parents of the past, the absence of time-saving machines and services, caused them to be more casual and less vigilant about their children's physical and mental well-being. But even the poorest, most harried parents today take health and safety precautions as a matter of course, visiting clinics, making efforts to prevent accidents, and so on. Perhaps the greatest indication of this new carefulness is the practice among working mothers of using the television set as an "electronic baby-sitter" to keep their young children out of harm's way while they are gone.

Once parents were infused with the new consciousness, they no longer allowed their children to wander about freely, to fall into fires, or drown in open wells, or be trampled by carriages, as happened not infrequently in the past. No longer could such accidents be ascribed to a vengeful Providence bringing down justice for the parent's own transgressions. The child's suffering was now revealed to parents in all its pathos, and parents began to make great efforts to prevent or at the very least mitigate it. The era of the babysitter (and ultimately the electronic baby-sitter) had begun.

The assiduous attention to children's needs in the increasingly child-centered family worked well from the child's point of view, far better than previous methods. The child developed physical, emotional, and intellectual strengths that allowed him to surpass, in many ways, children of the past. But a natural by-product of increased parental attentiveness appeared: children became more demanding. This, it must be understood, did not represent a change in the child's basic nature; the young child continued to follow the same developmental patterns he had always followed. His increased demands were an adaptation to the new permissiveness in child rearing, just as docility and submission had once been an adaptation to life-threatening brutality. For the child remained egocentric, as he had ever been. Just because his parents now gave him far more time and attention than ever before, he did not proceed to be "good" and check his natural impulses. On the contrary, the very fact that they had given him so much of what he desired made him demand even more.

This new demandingness, coupled with a vigor and precocity that stemmed from the optimal satisfaction of early needs, was further compounded by the increased parental time and effort required by modern child rearing. These factors contributed to the mid-century parental dilemma, which in turn paved the way for the widespread adoption of television as a way of life with young children.

The problem lay in the increasing inability of parents to manage their ever more demanding and able children with modern child-rearing methods based on the child's needs alone. Beating was out. Starvation was out. Even mild shaming and the gentlest terrorizing (Santa Claus won't bring you any presents if you don't behave) were frowned upon. But while the parents' needs for free time and relief had increased as a result of the increased burdens of child care, their opportunities to satisfy these needs in acceptable ways had diminished. Thus when television appeared, it was seized upon as a way out of the dilemma: a flick of the switch transformed the child completely, albeit temporarily, from an energetic, noisy, intrusive creature craving activity and experience and requiring constant supervision and attention, into a docile, quiet, undemanding presence. And this marvelous transformation was achieved with the child's cooperation! The child *wanted* to watch television, *loved* to watch, couldn't seem to have enough of it!

Perhaps it was the child's unprecedented complicity in his own pacification by television that allowed parents to employ it so relentlessly and so openly. Perhaps because encouraging a child to watch television was so easy and pleasant when compared to the more disagreeable or difficult strategies of the past, parents overlooked the fact that those very behaviors that cause them trouble, those explorations, manipulations, and endless experiments in cause and effect, are profitable and indeed necessary activities for a small child, and that dealing with children's difficult behaviors by eliminating them entirely via the television set is not dissimilar to suppressing a child's natural behavior by threats of physical punishment, and surprisingly similar to drugging a child into inactivity with laudanum or gin.

In addition to eliminating activities and behaviors in the child's life that are beneficial and necessary to his optimal development, television came to eliminate child-rearing behaviors on the parents' part that may have been equally important. For as parents grew to depend on television more and more in their daily lives with their children, they withdrew from an active role in their children's upbringing, and gradually became less and less capable of coping with their strong but undisciplined offspring.

Yet modern parents continue to use television in a drug-like way, concerning themselves primarily with the niceness or nastiness of the drug ("Batman" is bad; "Mr. Rogers" is good). When we consider that children spend three to seven hours of each day of the most formative years of their lives watching television, it begins to appear that the nightmare of child neglect has not ended, that after a brief and promising awakening, parents have drifted back into a destructive style of child rearing.

11

How Parents Survived before Television

Before television, in the thirties and forties, at the very height of the transformation of child rearing from a parent-centered to a child-centered business, the metaphysics of the new child-rearing philosophy was of necessity tempered by the empirical reality of everyday life with children. In order to survive, parents needed some time for themselves away from the incessant demands of their small children. Thus they were required to develop certain strategies, which, being parent-centered rather than child-centered, went somewhat against the modern grain. Although originating in the parents' needs, these proved to be of value to the child himself because they counterbalanced certain of the excesses of a child-centered upbringing.

Parents abandoned many of these disciplines when television presented itself as an easier alternative. In trying to assess the meaning of the television experience in children's lives today, it is important to consider what parents of the thirties and forties actually *did* when they simply *had* to get away from their children for a bit. By examining these courses of action we may discover what they offered the child, even as they offered the parent some relief.

Observing with an Eagle Eye

Before television the mother of a small child had a great need to develop her child's ability to play by himself for periods of time. But this was never a simple matter. The mothers had to find ways to ensure that the child would become truly involved in play for a time, leaving the mother to her own pursuits.

Thus the mother of the past was wont to observe her small children with an eagle eye to obtain a subtle picture of their changing development, not out of intellectual curiosity necessarily, but because this accumulation of information was useful to her in finding ways to get her children to entertain themselves successfully and reliably. A mother might take pains to discover, for instance, if her three-year-old was capable of learning to cut with a pair of blunted scissors. If this activity amused the child, it would be worth the mother's while to *work* on it a bit, to help the child learn how to cut properly, to provide a supply of colored papers or old magazines, a jar of paste perhaps, because her reward would be a self-entertaining child once the skill was acquired. For similar reasons the mother might provide buttons or beans for sorting, or dough for molding, or blocks for building, spurred not entirely by devotion to her child's happiness, but also by a certain amount of healthy self-interest.

Capturing her child's nascent interests and utilizing them to serve her own needs was once an important element for success as a mother. But as it happens the intimate knowledge of her child gained through sharp observation of his development necessarily led the mother to a more satisfying relationship with her child, with greater opportunities for shared pleasures as well as a reduced likelihood of misunderstandings and inadvertently inflicted suffering.

From the child's point of view the period of solitary play augmented by the mother's efforts to make sure that it actually "worked" led to the development of important skills and to actual, tangible accomplishments —constructions, drawings, sculptures, collages, animal parades, whatever. These skills and accomplishments, in turn, gave the child a sense of competence, and thereby helped to counteract those feelings of helplessness and utter dependence that dominate early childhood.

Indeed the heightened attentiveness to children's needs and interests that parents once displayed affected the entire family in a beneficial way. Parents became experts on their children, and the information inevitably enabled them to raise their children more humanely, more effectively.

Without doubt the availability of television as a child-rearing tool has reduced parents' immediate *need* to know their children well. Though still inspired by affection or a sense of duty to observe their children and communicate with them in a variety of ways, parents make diminished efforts to understand their children because their own needs are no longer a motivating force.

The Father as a Survival Aid

Before television another source of relief for a child-ridden mother appeared on her doorstep at five-thirty with a lunch pail or a briefcase. The father was once a traditional survival aid. Arriving home from his job, he was often greeted with a baby to feed or a child to play with. Though he often accepted this job with a certain reluctance, he found it a different kind of work than his daily labors, and more often than not he enjoyed it.

The mother dumped the kids on the father and went for a walk or took a bath or did some work or read a book. This was a course of action necessary for her survival and she was refreshed and replenished by it. The father was left to amuse the children. In order to preserve the peace and his sanity during his spells of child care, he had to discover his children's likes and dislikes, their weaknesses and strengths. In order to succeed as a caretaker, he was obliged to figure out how his children thought and why they behaved as they did. It is not hard to see that this knowledge gained by necessity would stand him in good stead in his future relationship with them, allowing him to form deeper bonds based on real experiences rather than on idealized images.

Children in such a situation are stimulated by learning to get along with a person who is not their principal caretaker, though an important part of the family.

Their interest is stirred by his new ways of behaving when he is actually in charge of them. They devise new strategies that do not work on their mother in order to get their way. They evolve new games and rituals to perform with their father that differ in important ways from those they play with their mother, routines that require time to develop.

Of course, taking care of small children is often a trying occupation for a father weary from a long work day. Though he has much to gain from playing with his children for regular periods each day, it is only natural that he would forgo these advantages were there an alternative child-minder available to allow him to settle down after work with a drink and a newspaper.

A mother reports:

"Whenever my husband spells me off with the kids he has them watching TV. That's his way of taking care of them, turning the TV on. He lets the networks do it for him."

Television offers an irresistible alternative to the weary father impressed into child care. But children suffer a serious deprivation as a result of this new strategy: fewer opportunities to establish and consolidate a relationship with their father.

The Nap

The most dependable survival aid for mother, however, was the nap. There was a time in the not too distant past when children took naps regularly during their entire early childhood, often until they began school. It wasn't necessarily that the child *needed* a nap, nor that he *wanted* a nap: he *had* to nap, quite simply. The nap was as inevitable and accepted a part of life as going to bed at night or getting dressed or brushing teeth or doing any of those many things that children don't particularly want to do but simply have to do in the course of their childhood.

The nap was inevitable because mothers needed that regular hiatus from child care. They saved up their telephone calls, their letter writing, reading, or sustained thinking for that interval of the day when an eye or an ear didn't have to be cocked in the direction of a small child.

Babies still spend the greatest part of their day sleeping, and children during their first two years continue to sleep for certain intervals during the day. But a great many of today's children give up napping during their third year, when they cease to physiologically require that daytime interval of sleep. This was the point when mothers of the past had to make a great effort to retain the nap. Since the child no longer fell asleep automatically at nap time, he naturally did his best to gain access to his mother's time and attention. This he did by "fussing," as mothers called it. But as a result of firmness based on a certain desperation and an almost physical need for time away from the child, mothers of the past persevered in their efforts to retain the nap, and the sleep nap gradually turned into a play nap, during which time the child was required to remain in his room, playing or dreaming or puttering about quietly. Mothers generally managed to retain the nap as a regular part of their daily routine until school brought the opportunity of a new daily break.

Today parents do not "work" to keep the nap. Instead, with relief in sight second only to the relief they feel when their child is asleep at night, parents work on their young children to encourage them to watch television for reliable periods of time, a far easier job than working on a child to stay in his room during a nap. Perhaps some of the child's deep affection for the television experience in his later years is rooted in his earliest experiences with the medium when his mother, seeing television as a survival aid, made special and seductive efforts to "plug him in."

Here a young, well-educated mother in need of relief from the hardships of life with a small child describes her efforts to establish her child on a television-watching routine:

"Last spring, when Jeremy was one and a half,

he gave up his morning nap. It was a difficult time, for him and for us. At that point I first started to try 'Sesame Street.' I made an effort to interest him in the program. I'd turn the set on and say, 'Look! There's a car!' or whatever. But he showed absolutely no interest. It really didn't seem worth working at then.

"Then, in the fall, when he was two, he gave up his nap entirely. The day loomed so long that I began to make another effort to interest him in 'Sesame Street.' He was more verbal then, and I thought there was a better chance that he'd understand it. I'd turn it on, and he'd show an initial interest in the first moments. It was an event. He'd look at it briefly, and then go on to other things. I'd leave it on and he'd pass by and look at it on his way to somewhere else. I might sit in front of it myself for a while, to try to make it more inviting, to try to coax him to watch. If he asked for a bottle, I'd certainly let him have it there, in front of the television set. Sometimes I'd even suggest a bottle.

"Anytime we were home and 'Sesame Street' was on, around four o'clock, I'd turn it on and try to interest him by commenting about things on the screen. 'Oh, look at the snow!' and things like that. Then I bought a book on 'Sesame Street' and we looked at it together. I think that helped get him interested. It took from about October to Christmas. Finally it 'took.' It was quite gradual. But now he watches every day, with a bottle, always, in the morning and in the afternoon. And 'Mr. Rogers,' too, most of the time, and it's really a great breathing spell for me.

"I know television probably isn't great for kids, but a few hours a day can't really be so bad. I suppose if I hadn't had a TV set I would have tried to establish some quiet-time routine in his room, a play-nap sort of thing. But it would have been hard. He's a very determined little boy. He probably wouldn't have stayed there."

In choosing television over the nap today's mother is following a simple imperative of human nature: always choose the easier of two possible courses of action, other things being equal. Pre-television mothers who persevered in enforcing a regular nap were operating on the same principle—in their case the harder alternative was to have a child underfoot all day. But is there an essential difference between these two "easier" courses, the nap and television watching? Probably, for when the child who took a regular daily nap throughout his early years outgrew the need for actually sleeping, the nap period began to serve a new function: it provided him with his first regular opportunity to experience free time. An understanding of the importance of free time in a child's life reveals how great a deprivation its loss may be.

12

Television and Free Time

A look back at some of the common routines once enforced by parents—regular naps, solitary play, and the like—reveals that children were once faced with regular periods of time they were required to deal with on their own. Today not merely are children's lives packed with a greater number of meetings, lessons, and other structured activities than ever before, but all the possible chinks of empty time cropping up between these activities are filled in with the mortar of television. That curiously unvalued commodity called free time has been eliminated almost entirely from children's lives.

Let us look at some children's daily routines:

James Harrison is 3 years old. He wakes up in the morning at seven o'clock, gets dressed with a little help, and watches "Captain Kangaroo" until breakfast. He spends the morning at nursery school. After arriving home from school, he eats lunch, watches "Sesame Street" and "Mr. Rogers" from one to two-thirty. Then his mother takes him to the park where he rides his tricycle and swings on the swing. From the park he goes shopping with his mother. He comes home, watches cartoons or "Sesame Street" again while his mother prepares dinner. After dinner, he plays a game with his father, watches "Zoom," has a bath, and goes to bed.

Margo Brown is 7. She gets up in the morning at seven-thirty, dresses, watches "Bugs Bunny," has breakfast, watches "Felix the Cat," and leaves for school. She comes home at three-thirty, changes into play clothes, and plays outside for an hour with her friends if the weather is good. If the weather is unpleasant, she and her friends watch television at one of their houses. At four o'clock on Monday afternoons she has a piano lesson. On Wednesday afternoons at four-thirty she goes to dancing class. Thursday afternoon is the Brownie meeting. On Fridays she stays after school for an arts and crafts program. She usually watches her favorite programs after her regular afternoon activities until her dinner is ready: "Batman," if she's home early enough, followed by "Superman," "The Brady Bunch," and sometimes "I Dream of Jeannie." Her older sister usually watches with her. After dinner she does her homework, practices the piano, and usually watches another television program before her bedtime at eight-thirty or nine (depending on the program)—either "Happy Days" "Little House on the Prairie," "The Waltons," or "Sanford and Son" (depending on the day).

Danny Evans is going on 14 and in the eighth grade. He gets up at seven, dresses, eats breakfast, looks at the sports page of the morning paper, and leaves for school at eight. He returns at four-thirty, grabs something to eat, and heads for the park where he plays ball with a regular group of friends every day. If it rains or if it's too cold, they play in a basement playroom in Danny's apartment house. When he comes home around five-thirty or six, he collapses in front of the television set and watches whatever his younger brother is watching, usually "Star Trek." He has dinner in the kitchen with his brother and little sister while watching television, since his parents eat later. The kids usually watch the "Partridge Family" or "Mod Squad" during dinner. After dinner he does homework, usually missing one of the programs the younger children watch, but sometimes he does his homework and half-watches at the same time. He often watches one more television program with his mother and father after the younger children have gone to bed, a movie or "Masterpiece Theater." His bedtime is around ten-thirty.

There is something these three children have in common with one another and with a great number of children in America: they have no free time.

Competing with TV

In many families parents fill up their children's free time as a direct result of a competition that has been set up with the television set. If they do not "do" something, the parents fear, the children will turn to the television set. Thus they expend gargantuan amounts of energy to deflect their children's interest from the mechanical rival. When energy flags or other duties call, the parents resort to television with a desperation that reveals their underdog position in the power struggle they are waging with the mechanical rival.

"The thing I notice is that I have to spend a lot of my time and mental energy avoiding television. I have to keep thinking up things to do to keep the kids from watching TV. Their normal inclination is to watch television when they have no scheduled activity, and only if I make some sort of effort can I keep them from doing it," reports a mother of three young children.

A mother of two boys aged 7 and 5 tells an interviewer:

"I can't stand the idea of families where the kids come home from school and turn on the TV. You never get to talk to your kids. But it's complicated, you see. I don't *need* the TV as a baby-sitter at three-thirty when the kids come home from school, so I don't want them to watch then. I *do* need it between five and seven when I'm making dinner. That's when I *want* them to watch. And they *do* watch television then. It certainly makes life a lot easier for me. The trouble is they want to watch at three-thirty also. And unless I dream up something terrific for them to do then, they don't just want to play. They pester and pester me to let them watch."

A Brooklyn mother reports:

"I spend the weekends driving the children around to places just to keep them from the TV. Two weeks ago I drove from Brooklyn to Hershey, Pennsylvania, just to get the kids away from the television set. That's an eight-hour drive!"

The following story, told by a nontelevision-watching New York mother, is a good example of the competition for a child's time that the television set often establishes:

"A few weeks ago I went to a hospital to visit a little boy with a broken arm, a six-year-old boy I really like. There was a television set at the foot of his bed and he had the controls at hand. His mother had told me that he was really looking forward to my visit, and yet the whole visit was dominated by the presence of the television set. I arrived with a couple of good story-books and I proceeded to read him a story but I quickly realized that the moment I or the story wasn't quite interesting enough, he was going to turn on that television set. And in fact every so often he *did* turn it on, just to see what was on. I went on desperately, reading stories, playing cards, and hangman and tic-tac-toe, telling jokes, because I was determined not to let that damn set win. I was definitely competing against that television set the whole hour I was there. I practically had to stand on my head, but I think I did win, but not a complete victory, only about seventy-five–twenty-five in my favor."

For some parents, competition with the television set reflects an underlying lack of trust in their children's capacity to amuse themselves. A New York mother of two children shows her understanding of the relationship between her use of the television set and her fear of unfilled time:

"I tell the kids, 'Get out of my hair and go watch television,' because I can't imagine their being on their own without something to *stimulate* them—I think that's why television is such a problem in our house."

A mother of two young children began to limit her children's television consumption to an hour a day. She tells an interviewer:

"I began to realize that the message I was giving him every time I broke down and said 'Yes you *can* watch one more program' was 'No, you're not able to do anything else with your head besides watch television.' The message was that I didn't think he had the *capacity* to do anything else with his time himself and so I was giving him an out with the television."

In many families, of course, children fill their free time themselves by turning on the television set. But even in those families that limit television watching, the competition parents engage in with the television set effectively eliminates free time in their children's lives. If either the television set or some competing activity is always available, there is never a time during the day when a child has "nothing to do."

"Nothing to Do"

What is the function of free time in a child's life? Wouldn't it be just as well if the child's life were so full of things to do that the whole question of having "nothing to do" would be eliminated?

There is a picture book by Russell Hoban called *Nothing to Do*[1] that shows the value of free time for a young child, as well as the problems parents face in regard to a child's unorganized time.

Hoban's book deals with little Walter Possum, a member of an endearing family of humanoid possums, who bothers his parents because he has "nothing to do." Father Possum tells Walter to "play with your toys." But Walter doesn't feel like it. The father assigns him a job—to rake the leaves. But Walter soon loses interest. The only activity that seems to relieve the tedium is quarreling with his sister Charlotte, a terrible pest.

When Mother Possum needs to clean the house, Father gives Walter a smooth brown stone and instructs him to rub it when he has nothing to do. It is a magic stone, Father tells him. "You have to look around and think while you're rubbing it, and then the stone gives you something to do."

Naturally, belief in the magic of the stone leads Walter to discover all manner of things to do. He finds a long-lost ball, he visits a friend, he dreams up a buried treasure game. He even devises a clever way to keep his irksome little sister from interrupting his game by presenting her with a stick that is also invested with putative magic powers. Besides having fun, he stays out of his parents' hair all afternoon.

Hoban's book, as is the case with all fine books for young children, contains guidance for parents as well as entertainment for children. The child needs help, suggests Hoban, in gaining access to his inner resources. The clever possum-parent, discovering that straightforward rejection of the "go find something to do on your own and don't bother me" variety only serves to exacerbate the child's dependent, clingy tendencies, encourages the child to find pleasure in his own inventiveness by making a game out of the very idea of thinking up things to do.

The possum-child is not really fooled—that is a crucial point (he proves it by using the same stratagem to get his sister to amuse herself). But still the magic stone works, though the child clearly understands that it contains no thoughts, that he himself is providing the good ideas.

What is that magic stone that Father Possum gave Walter? It is a necessary release, an embodiment of the idea that it is *all right* to be less dependent, that his parents are *permitting* him to act on his own, to use his time in his own way. This was what Walter required in order to be able to deal with his free time.

If Father Possum had given his son a different sort of magic device, a box, for instance, that glistened and gleamed, changed shapes and colors, and contained its own amusement, the parental purpose might have been equally served (to keep Walter out of the way). But were it the most entrancing source of entertainment, it would still have been an extension of the parent. Though fascinated by it, the child would have found in it no release from his helplessness, no source of growth or confidence in his own abilities. For that is the primary function of free time in a child's life, to provide the necessary opportunities for reducing his dependence and developing his separate self. This cannot happen in one or two or twenty grand epiphanies, but only through a gradual, day after day, year after year accumulation of free-time experiences, each providing a revelation so tiny, perhaps, that neither the child nor the parent recognizes it. Only through those free-time experiences, those self-propelled activities in which games are invented and dreams dreamed, will the child discover a self dependable enough to sustain him in place of those people and things he has been dependent on for so long. Without such experiences, the child will ultimately grow less dependent on his parents, but he may continue to remain dependent—on his peer group, on authority figures, on other experiences that allow him to remain a passive rather than an active participant in life.

Attachment and Separation

Television appears to have been instrumental in bringing about the demise of free time in children's lives. And yet, isn't television viewing itself a free-time activity?

The word "free" in the phrase "free time" is often accepted as a modifier of time, as if time were some real thing that has characteristics of its own apart from people or things, as if some kinds of time are "free," possessed of certain attributes of free-ness, while other kinds of time are not free. But time, of course, is not a corporeal thing. Its only reality is in relation to the person experiencing it. Free time, therefore, must be understood as defining the person experiencing that particular time, not the time itself; that is, free time is time when *a person is free* of certain limitations otherwise imposed upon his time, when he is able to act on his own volition, at his own pace, in his own way, free from all pressures and demands apart from those he invents.

And yet if a child's free time is defined as time when he is left to his own devices, free to fall back upon his own resources, then clearly there is a period at the beginning of life when those devices and resources must first be developed.

The infant does not differentiate between himself and his mother or the outside world. He has no "I" that is separate from others. His inner realities—hunger, fullness, pain, pleasure—merge with surrounding people and things in an overwhelming singleness of purpose: to live, to take in food, air, and a variety of visual, aural, and tactile sensory messages.

The developing child's first great task is to extricate himself from this undifferentiated mass and emerge as a *self*. A sign that this process has begun to occur comes when the infant ceases to treat his mother's comings and goings with equanimity. It is commonly observed that at about 7 or 8 months infants begin to howl and protest as if the world were coming to an end whenever their mother leaves the room. This behavior is an indication that the child has taken the first step in separating himself from his mother and the world at large. For only when the mother is perceived as a separate person can the infant grieve at her absence.[2]

The process of separation continues gradually during early childhood. Though the infant soon understands that he is physically separated from other people and things, there follows a period of time when he does not yet distinguish between his own feelings and objective reality. His understandings of the laws of physical causality, for instance, are almost totally egocentric and his own wishes and fears dominate his perceptions of reality. Those early years of life are indeed "magic years," when the child's inner world and the outside environment are still connected by primitive, irrational ties.[3]

A child's unoccupied time during those earliest years, the time not spent eating or sleeping or actively involved with a grown-up, is still governed by forces and pressures outside of his actual "self." Time cannot be free for a child for whom the events of time are so beyond control that it is only by chance that cause is ever followed by effect. The absence of a clearly defined self prevents the infant and very young child from manipulating his time in a free way; he is still in the thrall of a primary bondage to other people and things. The ability to communicate with language, to exercise control over his own body, to operate, in short, with some degree of independence, must be developed before the child can make use of time in his own way.

Most parents operate with an instinctive understanding of their child's need for a certain kind of time-filling during the first years of life. Knowing that the baby cannot gainfully employ his waking time to his own advantage, and realizing that the child's mental development is crucially affected by the nature of his human contacts during those gradually lengthening periods of waking time, parents intervene purposefully and to good effect during the first three years of life. That is to say, they cuddle the baby, dandle him, sing little songs to him, play games with his fingers and toes, rather than leaving him to his own devices.

Parents have also come to understand that the first attachment of the child to his mother or other nurturing adult, that attachment that resists separation with loud protests, serves to set the foundations for the child's future ability to love and nourish in his own right.

These understandings serve to make a child's time less than free during his first years. For it is clear that were the child left to his own devices and resources (whatever they might be), his rudimentary abilities and his developing personality would atrophy.

But quite a different situation exists when the child approaches the age of three. Now there is a distinct decline in the intensity of his attachment. He no longer grieves loudly and passionately when his mother leaves. He no longer clings to her for security in new situations. The emotional foundations have been laid, as it were, and a new developmental stage begins in which the child starts to explore his environment with increased interest and tenacity. The drive of curiosity begins to overtake the drive for security and dependence.

Of course, the attachment behavior does not altogether disappear. The child swiftly returns to the safety of his mother when he is frightened or hurt. But the symbiotic ties are weakened; he has taken his first steps toward independence. There is an evolutionary purpose to this behavior progression from a mother-centered, passive, receptive orientation to an environment-centered, active, learning style of life: the individual's survival in society is necessarily a function of active, adaptive behavior. Yet it is at this point in a child's development, somewhere between the ages of 2 and 3, that mothers are most likely to begin turning on the television set for their young children, filling in the empty spaces in the child's day with an experience that temporarily but inexorably returns him to a state of attachment and dependence.

The consequences for the child must be seen as a developmental setback. While watching television, the young child is once again as safe, secure, and receptive as he was in his mother's arms. He need offer nothing of himself while he watches, as he must do, for instance, when he plays with another child. He runs none of the small risks that his normal exploratory behavior entails: he won't get hurt, he won't get into trouble, he won't incur parental anger. Just as he is beginning to emerge from his infant helplessness, he is lured back into passivity by the enticements of the television set.

Free Time and Filled Time

Once a child reaches a stage at which he is capable of shaping time to his own needs, in choosing television he may fill empty time in a way that impinges upon his freedom and deprives him of those opportunities for recreation of his self that are available in the course of truly "free" time. Such time may be called "filled" time to distinguish it from free time.

The distinction between filled time and free time may best be illustrated by an example from real life:

A four-year-old boy has a regular rest period in his room after lunch. His room is equipped with toys, books, drawing materials, an easy-to-operate phonograph and records. There is a window that looks out on a street.

At one time he actually slept during his rest period —it was a true nap. Now he is likely to engage in a variety of activities he himself chooses. Today he begins with blocks, building a series of high towers. That morning at nursery school the tall and complicated rocket ship he had constructed out of blocks had been deliberately knocked down by another child. Now, in his own room, he destroys each of his own towers with a ruthless swipe, wreaking imaginary revenge on the morning's miscreant. He is in control now; he has devised a means of letting out his pent-up anger. Though he is only filling time during his rest period, he has shaped the time freely to suit his inner needs.

Next he attempts to build a bridge out of blocks. He has seen someone else construct an elaborate bridge, but his own bridge does not work—the blocks keep falling down. He can't figure out how to do it. He proceeds to form a bridge with his own body instead, arching his back in the air. His success at this activity compensates somewhat for his failure with the block-bridge. He has begun to understand and act upon a rudimentary principle: one's sense of well-being depends upon a certain amount of success; failure makes one feel bad. Had he continued to work on the bridge until he had solved the architectural problem, he might have learned a different lesson, one to do with the relation of perseverance and hard work to success. Instead he went in a different direction.

Tiring of his acrobatics, he puts on a record and lies on his bed to listen. It is a record he has heard at least a hundred times. He reaches out for a special pillow with a soft cover and sucks his thumb while stroking the pillow with his fingertip. He half-listens to the record. The other part of his mind is somewhere else, somewhere soft and hazy and comfortable. He recognizes the feeling well, having traveled to that place many times. But he is dimly aware of a change. As he strokes and sucks and listens, occasional words and images of real things begin to enter the vague nothingness—thoughts, associations, ideas. Every once in a while he removes his thumb to inspect it, plays with his other fingers, tries to suck another finger to see if the pleasure is the same.

When the record is finished he goes to turn another on, but becomes interested instead in the turntable. He puts a piece of paper on it and watches it go round and round. Soon he has devised an entire game with little bits of paper going around on the turntable. It is *his* game, having come from an idea in his head. Then his mother comes in. The rest period is over.

The child has experienced a period of time he was free to manipulate in his own way. His use of time, free from all structures and pressures, was a step in the direction of self-discovery.

Consider another child whose empty time between lunch and the afternoon outing is filled with several hours of television viewing. His time is indeed filled by the television experience, but while he is engaged with the program he is free to do nothing but watch and listen. His will is nonexistent; his personal pace and needs are irrelevant. He does not think his own thoughts while watching television as he does when devising his own games; his mind is being "thinked for" by the television program. In a sense his relationship with the television program might be described as a return to that original, undifferentiated one-ness of infancy, so thoroughly do the child and the television image fuse into a single entity. As he watches the screen, the boundaries between inside and outside grow dim and vague, not unlike his state in the not-so-distant past when his self was still merged with the world and a single other. He has little power over time as he watches television. That particular aggregate of genetic endowment and adaptive behavior that defines the child's new self comes into play far less when he watches television than when he is engaged in any other activity. Indeed, the self is frequently obliterated, temporarily but completely, as the child descends into a trancelike state of consciousness.

Of course, not all the child's time should be unstructured and unconstrained by others even after he has reached the stage when he can profit from free time. There are things to learn and skills to acquire that require him to place his time in the hands of others. But he must have *some* free time to control if he is to prosper. With television in his home, that is precisely what he does not have.

Paradise Lost

If the child's access to free time plays an important part in his development, and if the prevailing attitude toward children today is centered around fulfilling the child's own needs, why do parents insist on filling their children's time so relentlessly?

A partial explanation lies in the difficult transition the mother must make as the child moves from its first all-encompassing attachment to the next stage of development. At this juncture it is natural for mothers to fret about the child's new independent activities. Whereas the child once clung to her and followed her about like a puppy, now she must pursue the child and keep him out of trouble. Moreover, with the intense attachment period still so vivid in her mind, the mother tends to feel rejected by the child's growing involvement with the world around him. Her subliminal sense of Paradise Lost as her supreme importance diminishes makes this a difficult period for her. Since her relationship with the child is rapidly changing, she must find new ways of dealing with the child's higher activity level while coping with her own feelings of loss. Ideally the mother will make changes in her daily procedures that will not work at cross-purposes with the child's developmental needs.

Perhaps it is partly the mother's ambivalent feelings about the child's new independence that compels her to use television to fill his time. Instead of adjusting to the child's emotional separation and craving for activity, she effectively limits her child's involvement with the outside world and prevents him from making new attachments by delivering him to the passive experience of the television set. Perhaps she feels that since she alone cannot entertain her child and make him happy, she will supply a substitute in the form of the television set. Thus she hangs on to her illusion of remaining the center of her child's universe, as indeed she so recently was. Thus she retains her supremacy in spite of the child's burgeoning independence, and in spite of his efforts to find an identity separate from hers.

The Easy Out

But the more obvious explanation of why parents of young children turn to television is that it presents the *easiest* and most reliable relief from the increasing difficulties of child care. The strategies once used by parents to survive life with small children simply seem too much trouble to parents today.

A mother notes:

"When I had Sally and we didn't have a TV set I guess I felt less pressures to do other things, because I had no choice. If she needed attention and I was making dinner I said, 'Oh, to hell with dinner—we'll just eat fifteen minutes later,' and I'd sit down and read her a story or get her started off playing with something. But when Henry was born and we had a television set, I started using it more. It offered an easy out, and it replaced some sort of effort on my part."

This easy out does not merely allow the parent to make less effort; it also provides an occupation that is quiet and unobtrusive. This is why great numbers of parents feel they couldn't survive life without Saturday morning cartoons.

A mother of three boys says:

"I practically beg them to turn on the television set on Saturday mornings so they'll be quiet and I can sleep. When they play with each other they're just too noisy. They always play Emergency and love making the siren noises—*Weeeeoweeeowee!* When they play with each other every toy is out, every hat is on, every truck is moving—I suppose that's fine, but I can't stand it! I need my sleep! The six-year-old is usually up at the crack of dawn, and if it weren't for TV, he'd be playing with all the toys, too. But now he turns on the set and watches quietly until nine, when we get up."

The immediate benefits parents gain from the instant child-pacifying powers of the television set may prove costly in the long run. A look at some of the results of parental use of television suggests that the parents' lot is ultimately made harder, not easier, because of their use of television to fill in their children's time.

The Half-Busy Syndrome

An illustration of the counterproductive consequences of relying on television to fill the empty chinks in a child's day is seen in a combination of circumstances that might be called the *half-busy syndrome*. This describes a cycle in which the mother is *half*-busy *all* the time. She goes about her various duties and occasional leisure-time activities in bits and spurts, stopping whatever she is doing to take care of this or that, answering the child's persistent questions, taking make-believe tastes of endless mud-pies, admiring drawings. She is busy, but never too busy to look up from her book or stop her work to attend to the child's needs or wishes.

She becomes hardened to the half-busy way of life and finds a certain satisfaction in the idea that she is a "good mother." But occasionally she feels she must have some relief from being constantly "on tap." The television set suddenly seems the only solution.

She feels a bit guilty about using the television set as a baby-sitter, but what else is she to do? She has tended, minded, soothed, coaxed, and displayed the patience of seven saints. She must get away somehow.

After all, children are children and it is their nature to seek attention. She does not know that there is something about her state of "half-busy-ness" and perpetual availability that actually works against her own needs, making her child *more* demanding and creating the necessity of turning to the television set for relief.

Parents intuitively understand that children's behavior bears some relation to their own availability. For instance, it is universally observed that children are particularly troublesome when their mothers are on the telephone. But this is assumed to be an isolated phenomenon. Mothers who devote great *quantities* of attention to a child in the course of each day do not generally understand that the *quality* of that attention is a crucial factor.

Research findings suggest that the quality of a parent's attention matters considerably. In one experiment a selected group of preschool children was left for a period of time with a consistently available and attentive adult, while a second group spent a similar period of time with an adult who pretended to be busy with his own work. The children in the "low availability" condition proved to be considerably more demanding of the researcher's attention than the group whose caretaker was consistently available. The quality of the available caretaker's attention seemed to allow the children to play more independently and make fewer demands on him. The caretaker who seemed to be busy was far more beleaguered.[4]

A later research study observed nursery-age children with their mothers, some of whom were instructed to be busy and some to be wholly attentive. The results showed that many more bids for maternal attention were made when the mother was busy than when she was completely available to the playing child.[5]

Thus it appears that a reduction of free time in the child's life leads to an increase in dependence. For clearly the child whose mother is half-busy all the time is never more than half-free himself. He is never presented with the real necessity of confronting time in his own way. Whatever the reasons the mother feels compelled to be involved in *all* the child's time, if only in a partial way, the result of this behavior for her is disastrous: she is deprived of any truly free time for herself. And a reverse process may very well operate here: a mother deprived of free time grows dependent upon her child for emotional gratification that might better come from other sources.

The experiences of mothers who have changed the quality of their attentiveness confirm the likelihood that being half-busy throughout the day makes children more demanding and dependent. When periods of complete attention are alternated with periods of nonavailability to the child, both mother and child begin to enjoy truly free time.

A mother of two preschool children reports:

"One day I realized that I had fallen into the habit of caring for the children in a halfway sort of manner all the time. I'd get half a letter written and then have to stop because a child needed something. It went on that way most of the day and I'd never get away completely except when I plopped them in front of the television. I hated doing that, but I just couldn't help it. I needed to get away. Then I began to realize that I was in a sort of vicious circle, not really doing my own things, and not really enjoying the children very much either. Meanwhile I had a sinking feeling that time was passing, that there were only so many years when the children would be small, and that somehow I was never really completely committed to them, nor was I ever completely free of them.

"I was late coming to this realization and I actually had to work hard to make a change. It might have been easier if I had started right from the start. But of course when they were babies they needed a different sort of attention, didn't they? What I wanted to do now was *to really be with them* when I was with them, not just give them half of my attention. I'd drop everything for a while and really play with them, *down on the floor* much of the time. I wouldn't keep trying to get back to my letter or doing something else.

"But the other part of it was that I worked on getting away just as completely, without plugging them into the TV. It seemed somehow fair that if I gave them my time completely, they could also give me some time completely to myself. I didn't even think then that they would profit from having time entirely to themselves. But in fact I began to realize that often that was the case. I'd tell them that I was going to do something for a while and they could not interrupt me, and that when I was finished I'd do something with them. And then *I stuck to my guns!*

"I started out little by little, because they wouldn't let go at first. I'd say, 'I'm going to sit here and read to the bottom of the page.' And then I'd persist, no matter what they did, even though it meant ignoring things like falling down or a fight. It never got to a life-or-death situation—I suppose I would have intervened then. Gradually I increased the time I was unavailable to them, slowly, page by page.

"It worked. In fact, it was pretty easy. Now they will really give me time, without demanding attention or getting attention in devious ways—by getting hurt, for instance, or by making a horrible mess. Somehow, my giving them honest-to-goodness attention really seems to make a difference. It seems to fill them up, in a way, almost as if they've had enough to eat. They become calmer, less clingy. They seem to be more capable of being on their own for longer periods of time."

Waiting on Children

When television is used to fill in children's free time, parents are often led to compensate for lost opportunities to become close to their children by waiting on them more than they might ordinarily do. It might surprise a great number of parents to learn that the many little services they provide children who could easily help themselves are debilitating to the children. They might be even more surprised to realize that their compulsion to wait on their children is related to the role television plays in their family life.

There have always been parents who like to "baby" their children unnecessarily. Literature is full of horrendous models of such parents who perform ridiculous services for their perfectly capable (and usually ungrateful) offspring and openly struggle to hold on to their children by keeping them mentally and physically dependent.

But the mothers who fetch drinks and snacks for their television-watching children, who release them from their chores so that they may watch their favorite programs, are not all Mrs. Portnoys. While the infantilizing effects on their children's development may be similar, their motives for waiting on their children are frequently related to their use of television as a surrogate parent.

An illustration of the relationship between children's television watching and parents' waiting on children is given by Caroline L., a musician and the mother of two school-age children:

"I've scheduled my life and my work in such a way that I can be there when the children come home from school. I want to be of some help to them, to greet them, to make them feel good in some way. Well . . . [she laughs with embarrassment] I regret to say that they plunk themselves in front of the television as soon as they come home, and sometimes I can barely get two sentences out of them before they're involved in their program. Then I can't get another word out of them. And so I bring them some carrot sticks or Triscuits and cheese for a snack, feeling a little ridiculous about it, because they're certainly old enough to peel their own carrots and make their own snacks. But somehow I allow myself to do it. I mean, if they love those television programs so much . . ."

Caroline L. brings her children snacks because she can think of no other way to maintain communication with them as they watch television. She feels rejected, cut off from normal human contact with her children. Moreover, she feels guilty that she set up this situation herself, by using the television regularly for her own convenience when the children were smaller.

She is aware of her dependence on the television set when she notes her alternatives, as she sees them:

"The funny thing is, when they come home from school I really have a desire to sit down and talk to them about what they're doing in school. I'd love to hear about that. But they don't want to talk about it. I'm sure if I were willing to do something with them in the afternoon, something they really like, at least there would be a chance they'd be willing to do that instead of watch TV. Maybe not. But I'd have to completely devote my time to entertaining them, even to the extent of not answering the phone. And that's really hard for me. I've tried."

In this way countless parents whose normal communications with their children have been damaged by the television set, who are regularly "turned off" by their children in favor of the television set (just as they "plugged in" their children when they were younger), now perform unnecessary little services to manifest their love and devotion, to show their children in deed rather than word that they care for them and want them to be happy. That is the only possibility left to them, they feel, since their words have been preempted by television's electronic words.

A child psychotherapist and consultant for a New York private school comments on the effects of waiting on children:

"It's a very infantilizing thing for mothers to wait on children, clear away their dishes, bring them drinks and little snacks while the children sit there watching television. Long after children reach an age when they ought to begin to develop self-reliance, they can't help but continue to regard their parents as servicing people. Of course, babies don't see their parents as servicing people—they *need* to be taken care of. But when seven- or eight-year-old children habitually ask their parents to fetch them a glass of water because they're watching a television program, and the parents meekly comply, then there's something unwholesome going on.

"The parents rarely bring this up as an issue, however," notes the therapist. "I just pick it up as they're talking. They'll be describing a certain situation and they'll mention that so-and-so called them to bring him a sandwich—that he's watching TV—and so-and-so is ten years old!" There is a certain amount of wonder in the therapist's voice as she relates this incident.

"The parents feel guilty about allowing their children to watch so much television," she continues, "and so they try to compensate by waiting on their children. It's not that they are trying to keep them dependent, as parents sometimes do. But these parents just don't seem to know what else to offer. Somehow they have come to think that *they* have to do all the offering. That's what astonishes me."

Drifting

If one were to seek the effects of the large-scale reduction of free time among a generation of children growing up with television, an understanding of the importance of free time in children's lives would lead one to look for signs of increased dependence. A few experienced observers of children have, indeed, begun to observe such signs.

For example, the founder and director of an excellent children's camp in Vermont began to observe a curious increase in homesickness in the early sixties. There had always been a small number of campers afflicted with homesickness, but now an epidemic seemed to have struck. The camp had devised a number of successful strategies for combating homesickness, and these were now applied with equal success. Nevertheless the increased incidence of homesickness continued to be a problem year after year. When the director checked with counselors from other camps, he learned that they had not encountered a similar problem. It was a mystery. Perhaps the answer would be found in some aspect of life at his camp that differed from other camps.

There was indeed one great difference: while other camps filled every minute of the campers' day with programmed activities, rests, and meals, this particular camp interspersed its programmed activities with four half-hours during which the children were free to pursue their own interests. These were called "drifting" periods. The camp director had deliberately structured a program that combined planned activities with free periods, believing that the opportunities provided by the free-time periods were as important for the children as those planned for them. Whatever growth took place during the camp months, he felt, depended as much on the child's deployment of the drifting periods as on his success at the programmed activities. However, he and his staff could not fail to observe that homesickness was most acute during those free-time periods.

The camp had been running in very much the same way, with the same sort of staff and the same population of middle- and upper-middle-class children, for over twenty years. Why now, starting in the mid-sixties, were the free-time periods making numbers of children sufficiently uncomfortable to feel homesick?

Since the youngest children at the camp were aged nine, the first television-bred children would have arrived in camp in the mid-sixties. These were children who had far less experience of free time in their lives than previous generations. When suddenly confronted with regular doses of free time, they reacted with anxiety and homesickness.

For homesickness is always a cry against a surfeit of independence, a cry to return to a more dependent situation in which the child need not function as a separate self. It represents a longing to return to that cozy family group of which the child was once an actual physical appendage, and from which he must, someday, extricate himself emotionally if he is to grow up successfully.

When a child's opportunities to experience free time are limited, he is more likely to remain in a state of inner dependence. While his life is completely filled with adult-devised programs on television, his dependence will not be apparent, for he is spared the need to act independently. But when he is forced to confront unstructured time, as the campers were, he will find himself resourceless. His dependence will be exposed.

A New Gresham's Law of Child Activity

It is all very well to sing the apotheosis of free time for children and exhort parents to turn off their television sets. It is the *reality* of free time that makes it so difficult for parents to stick to their resolve to limit their children's television consumption.

The situation modern parents face upon turning off the television set frequently proves to be discouraging. After expecting their offspring to suddenly metamorphose into Victorian children who pursue hobbies and wholesome adventures, it is depressing to see them hanging around doing nothing. In a variety of rude ways the children reject those fine, creative activities with which they are supposed to fill the vacuum, challenging the parents to either amuse them themselves or relent and let them watch television.

Is it partly or wholly because of their early television experiences that children today are less capable of dealing with free time? Do they have greater difficulties in combating boredom than children did in the pre-television era?

A sort of Gresham's Law of Child Activity seems to operate here: passive amusements will drive out active amusements. Since passive amusements require less effort than active ones, human nature dictates that, all other things being equal, doing something easier is preferable to doing something harder.

Observe a child playing with a simple wooden truck who is presented with a complicated mechanical locomotive. Whereas he had been obliged to amuse himself by pushing the symbolic vehicle around the floor, devising an imaginary route in and out and under furniture (providing his own sound effects), now he watches the new toy with fascination, amazed by the smoke spouting from the stack, charmed by the rhythmic toot-toot of the engine, delighted by its ability to propel itself backward and forward.

But after a while the child's pleasure in the new toy begins to diminish. The fascinating toy, after all, has a limited repertory of actions: it moves, blows smoke, and goes toot-toot. The child wrings a terminal bit of amusement from the toy by taking it apart to see how it works. And it is finished.

The child's play with the simple wooden truck does not lead to a similar habituation because its range of activities is limited only by his own imagination.

But now the troublesome aspect of Gresham's Law of Child Activity becomes apparent: for though the attractiveness of the mechanical plaything is brief, there is something so compelling about the passive pleasure it affords the child that the appeal of another toy requiring active participation is diminished. When the mechanical toy breaks down, the child is not likely to go back to his wooden truck. That sort of play seems a bit dull and tame, a bit *difficult* now. How silly it seems to push a truck around the house and pretend that it's real when a painted truck that moves on its own is so much *realer!*

Not only will the child choose this particular mechanical toy over the more effort-demanding symbolic toy it was meant to replace, but in the future he will tend to choose a passive occupation over an active one. Passive play experiences inevitably make active play less appealing, and therefore less likely to occur spontaneously.

The television set is the one mechanical toy that does not lead easily to habituation and boredom, though the child's involvement with it is as passive as with any other mechanical toy. It chugs and toots and produces movements, while the child watches with wonder. But its actions and sounds are far less repetitive than the toy train's, so the watching child can maintain wonder and fascination almost indefinitely.

But just as the ordinary mechanical toy changes a child's relationship to symbolic toys, so do the passive pleasures of television watching transform his relationship to his own time. The strong pleasures of that safe, effortless, ever-amusing experience make the pleasures afforded by active entertainments seem too much like *work*.

This is not to say that normal children will stay huddled before the television all day in preference to playing baseball or going to a game with their father or baking a chocolate cake or engaging in some other appealing activity. Certain activities will always confound Gresham's Law of Child Activity by dint of their special attractions: special trips and activities, particularly with parents, beloved sports and games, activities that dovetail with the child's special interests. But those activities have got to be *pretty good*. Otherwise there's always television.

"TV is a killer of time for my children," reports a mother. "I think they'd almost rather do *anything* than watch TV. If I find them something they like to do and do it with them, they're perfectly happy. They'd prefer that to watching TV. It's just so much less effort to watch TV than to have to think of something to do. So if they don't have something *special* to do, like getting a Halloween costume ready or even going to a friend's house, their first thought is to watch TV."

Another mother says:

"What I find with my seven-year-old is that it's the *excuse* of television, the very *presence* of the television set when he doesn't know what to do with himself, or when he has a day when another child isn't coming over to play, that keeps him from looking to himself for something to do. Instead, he'll want to sit in front of the television set just to let something come out at him. That's been the hardest thing about television for me. If the television were not there, if it didn't exist, he wouldn't have that problem."

A mother of a five-year-old boy observes:

"My child is not the kind of child who will make a scene or have a temper tantrum. He'll just mope around and be bored. And I find it very hard to take that. It bothers me to think that he can't do anything with his time. The presence of the television is the excuse. He knows in the back of his mind that when he really hits rock bottom he can go to that television set."

An educator and authority on early childhood with forty years of experience as teacher and principal has noted a change in children's behavior since the advent of television:

"Young children today have a sophistication that comes from all their contacts with the outside world via television, but sophistication and maturity are not the same thing.

"Children today are often *less* mature in their ability to endure small frustrations, or to realize that something takes a longer time to do, that it isn't *instant*. They're less tolerant of letting themselves become absorbed in something that seems a little hard at first, or in something that is not immediately interesting. I spend a lot of time at school telling children that they have to participate in activities and try things even if something doesn't seem all that interesting right at the start."

Other teachers observe that young children today find it harder to work by themselves than children did in the pretelevision era, that there is a constant need for adult supervision or entertainment.

Whether children are so used to immediate gratification via the television set that their abilities to amuse themselves have atrophied, or whether a simple lack of experience with free time has left them with undeveloped abilities, it nevertheless seems clear that children today have greater difficulty dealing with free time than children of past eras.

For when those favorite, special activities are not available (as often is the case, which is what makes them so special), then children today are not likely to enlarge their interests by trying something new. They will not take the same desperate measures to combat boredom that children of the past had need to resort to: inventing games, playing make-believe, reading, rereading, writing to pen pals, pursuing hobbies—activities that grow on a child and make him grow. With the presence of a source of passive amusement in every home, readily available to the child at the first sign of boredom, a child's time becomes more and more dominated by this single time-suspending activity.

Sickness As a Special Event

Before television there were occasions in almost every child's life when he was faced with a great deal of unexpected free time: those inevitable days when he was removed from his normal schedule of activities by sickness.

Most adults today who grew up before television have strong memories of their childhood illnesses.

A mother thinks back:

"My mother worked when I was a child, but when I was sick she stayed home for at least a few days. So I remember those times very well. I remember the endless card games, and playing Hangman hundreds of times, and cutting out pictures from magazines with her. I remember lying in bed and calling her to come and bring me this or that, again and again and again. And I remember how wonderful it felt, that she always came! I suppose I ran her ragged, but that's a very important memory for me, to this day."

Another parent relates:

"I remember being excruciatingly bored when I was sick. But that boredom sometimes led to odd activities. I'd make up stories and illustrate them, out of sheer desperation. Or I'd decide to learn French by reading the French dictionary. (I only got to page three.) Or I'd look through old photograph albums and daydream about life in the old days."

It is remarkable how often the actual physical discomforts of sickness are absent from these childhood memories, although a child's sickness is in reality dominated by symptoms and the mental changes that accompany them: fever, nausea, weakness, coughing, itching, pain, accompanied by restlessness, insecurity, depression, and other aberrations or exaggerations of the child's normal mental state.

But while the adult's memory may linger upon the romantic aspects of his childhood illnesses—the confirmation it afforded of parental devotion, the creative ferment it often inspired—at the time it was a tedious reality for his parents. Parents have always dreaded the days when their children are sick. It is distressing enough for parents to suffer the natural anxiety that a child's sickness provokes, the sharp reminder of his vulnerability and mortality; the child's sudden reversion to dependency and his need for steady services compound the unpleasantness. The parents' pity and sympathy for the child's discomfort are invariably tempered with impatience and weariness at his temporarily more difficult behavior.

Television has transformed the experience of sickness for parents and children in America. It is a more effective drug than aspirin in ameliorating the symptoms of disease. Television makes the time pass more quickly, and the child concentrates less on the stomachache, the general malaise, the itching, or whatever wretchedness the particular infliction has visited upon him. The relief is felt equally strongly by the parent, who formerly bore the burden of helping the child pass time and keeping his mind off his physical discomforts. Gone are the onerous requirements of time and patience on the parent's part—the endless story readings, the tedious card games ("I thought I'd go mad if I had to play one more game of War"), the listening to whiny complaints, the steady need to restrain impatience, to maintain sympathy, to act more lovingly than ever.

But however tiresome and unpleasant sickness may have been all around, being sick was undoubtedly a special event in pre-television days. Then a child did special things, had special relationships with his parents and siblings. And in a curious way the specialness of sickness helped define the normalities of life for children. The elongation of time in the sick bed changed the child's concept of normal time and helped him to develop a rudimentary understanding of the relationship between time and activity. The opportunities that sickness afforded a child for a more contemplative relationship with his parents frequently exposed both to new aspects of the other's personality. Best of all, from the child's viewpoint, the usual sibling battle was suspended when he was sick. Parents no longer had to take pains to be "fair" about their allocation of time or affection: sickness was special, and parents were able to bestow on the sick child giant doses of time and affection without fear of provoking mutinous jealousy among his siblings (in fact, their jealousy was merely repressed, something not lost on the sick child and treasured in later memory).

Since the advent of television, the times a child is sick are special only inasmuch as he is allowed to watch more television than ever.

"When the children are sick I'm likely to let them watch all they want," says a mother who normally limits her children's television viewing. "Otherwise I'd have to read to them all day. Also, it's slightly making up to them for the miserable time they're having."

"When the kids are sick it's permissive time so far as the television is concerned," another mother observes. "Usually we're pretty strict about television, but when they're sick I feel they ought to have a special treat, somehow. Although," she adds thoughtfully, "it's a little odd to make a treat of something I normally disapprove of. But it's too tempting not to let them watch."

It is almost cruel to suggest that a parent faced with the mental and physical rigors of coping with a sick child not take advantage of a mechanical aid to ease the task. But the parent ought to reflect on the consequences for the child: a "special event" of childhood made ordinary and forgettable, an opportunity lost for strengthening family relations. Moreover, the strangeness and unreality of illness is exaggerated by hours of television fantasy. Though the mother's lot is made easier, there is no question but that those stories read, those card games played, those quiet times together, enrich the child's life, and are an especial loss for today's child whose television viewing has already cut down on shared experiences with his parents.

The Disappearance of "Real Life"

In the not too distant past children were expected to be passive participants in their school experiences. The idea used to be that the teacher had a body of material to teach that children were to soak in as part of a process called "learning." In this one-way process any activity on the children's part other than that specifically directed by the teacher was considered inappropriate.

Much of the success of this educational system depended on the personality of the teacher. If he was wise and kindly and graced with that indefinable charisma characterizing gifted teachers and performers, then children, like the audience at a good play, would try to conform to his rigorous behavior requirements and thus manage to soak in the required information. If the teacher possessed none of these gifts, very little learning occurred.

When school let out in the old days, children ran amok. Outside the boundaries of the schoolroom they ran, played games, dreamed, plotted, planned, yelled like Indians, skipped stones, started fires, made fences, baked cookies, rolled in the mud—played freely. Once school was over, children took charge of their own activity.

Within the last decade a change has been taking place in the classroom. Children are being encouraged to initiate, to explore, to manipulate, and the one-way process of education has been shifting to an interactive situation between the teacher and the child. Children are no longer bound by rigid codes of behavior, but are allowed to move freely, to talk naturally to each other and to the teacher in the course of their school activities. The success of this new style of education depends less on the teacher's charismatic personality and more on his intelligence and intuition, as well as on the equipment available in the classroom for the children's manipulations and explorations. As in the past, some children learn and some children resist. But in either case the children spend their school day in a more natural state of activity.

The atmosphere at three o'clock is calmer today. When school lets out, kids no longer behave like creatures let out of cages. In their child-centered classrooms they seem to have released an adequate amount of energy. But for many of these children activity is just about over for the day. They head for home to settle down in front of their television sets. They watch the screen and passively soak in images, words, and sounds hour after hour, as if in a dream.

It might seem to even out. If school has become an active experience, then why shouldn't the child spend a few passive hours watching television? The answer is that no matter how child-centered and "free" a school situation may be, it is still organized and goal-centered. The child hasn't the freedom of choice and freedom to control his own time that he has after school, when he can play a game or not, throw stones or not, daydream or not. Though the hours in a modern classroom may be more active, more amusing, less punitive and repressive than in the old-fashioned classroom, the child is still being manipulated in certain directions, by the teacher, by the equipment in the classroom, by the time organization of the day. If he spends his nonschool time watching television, *that* time is also being effectively organized and programmed for him. When, then, is he going to live his *real life?*

13

Hooked Parents

Television arrived on the scene as a *deus ex machina* to help the beleaguered parent survive the rigors of modern child rearing. But as television replaced other strategies, parents found themselves increasingly unable to bring up their children without resorting to its use.

A mother of three children admits:

"I'm afraid not to have a television set even though I know the kids would probably be a lot better off without it. What would I do when I needed it? I'd just go to pieces. I can't imagine managing without it. I'm hooked on using it."

Why Parents Get Hooked

Two factors combine to "hook" parents on using television: its unique ability to pacify children and its ready availability.

It may seem obvious that when children watch television they are less troublesome to their supervisors than when they engage in normal play. Nevertheless a research study was devised and carried out to establish the truth of just such a hypothesis.

The study set out to answer these questions: Are children quieter while viewing television than while playing? What kinds of activities are engaged in during television viewing relative to the kinds of activities occurring during ordinary play time? Is there less need for parental control and supervision during television viewing than during play?

A team of trained observers visited a selected number of young children in their homes and compared their behavior while watching television with their conduct while playing with another child. The following acts were noted and scored when they appeared, either while the child watched television or while he played: talking, laughing, crying, sitting, walking, running, self-stimulation (rubbing the body, playing with hair, sucking a finger, etc.), aggression toward another person, destructive play, leaving the room. Controlling behavior on the part of the mother was also noted when it occurred.

The results of the study revealed that notably different behaviors occurred in the course of each condition—viewing and playing. Television viewing proved to be associated with more sitting, less walking, less talking, fewer attempts to leave the room, less aggression toward others, and, most important, less need for maternal interference.[1]

The simple presence of the set is an important factor in parents' growing dependence on television. It is *there* at all times, in every home (sometimes in every room). When the parent is faced with annoying behavior on the part of a child, the temptation to resort to television is strong, far stronger than if it were not so handy, easy to use, and swiftly effective.

A New York City mother of two young children reports:

"My husband is definitely more concerned about the children's television watching than I am. He thinks it prevents them from thinking. Well, maybe he's right, but I think being with children all day gives you a different attitude than if you only see them evenings. If you've had a hectic day and they want to go to their room and watch TV and leave you alone, well, you're not going to say, 'Don't do that. It's not intellectually stimulating.' You'll say, 'Fine. I want some peace.' I think that's something you don't understand unless you spend all day with the kids. My husband would say, 'You shouldn't give in like that. We've set up the rules about TV and they should stick to them.' But men who are not with children all day don't understand. Sometimes when you're exhausted, it's a lot easier to give in."

A working mother of a three-year-old describes a similar situation:

"I come home at a quarter to five and I'm really beat. I just need to sit down, look at my mail, and collapse for a few minutes before dealing with my daughter. 'Mr. Rogers' allows me to do that. He's on at five. I use that program to give me a little space after work, even though I really agree that television watching isn't great for preschool children, and I tell parents at my school the same thing all the time. But 'Mr. Rogers' is better than other programs. I like the concentration on the self-worth angle. Still, that's not why I turn it on, to be honest about it."

How Parents Get Hooked

Interviews with mothers reveal a pattern of growing dependence upon television as a child-rearing tool. This occurs even when the mother does not start off using television to suit her own purposes but introduces it for the child's sake alone:

"When I first started turning on the television for the children," relates a Denver mother of two preschool girls, "it wasn't out of need, but because I thought it was a good thing to offer. I'd turn on the television set and say, 'It's time for "Sesame Street,"' even if it meant interrupting the girls in the middle of play. They didn't need to be coaxed to watch television. They enjoyed watching, and I often watched with them.

"But after a time television took on a different aspect in our household. The change was subtle, but looking back now, it's clear that a real change did take place. I suppose it was because I discovered how dependable an amusement television was, more dependable than any other. After a time whenever things came up, tiny domestic emergencies—when I had to talk to somebody on the phone, or when somebody dropped in, or when Marty called that he was bringing somebody home for dinner—that sort of thing—then I would turn to television for help.

"Suddenly I realized that I was no longer using television as an experience to offer the children, but as something with value for me. But by now it was hard to change my operating procedure. Now I no longer had to remind the children that it was time for their program, or interrupt them in their play. They really *wanted* to watch and were quite unwilling to find other amusements when I wasn't able to play with them myself."

Another mother reveals a similar ambivalence about her use of television:

"When he first started watching 'Sesame Street,' I was the one who started it. He went to school in the afternoons, and I'd put 'Sesame' on in the mornings, from nine to ten, I guess it was. I wanted him to watch it. I thought it was a good program, that he'd learn his numbers—you know, an educational kind of thing. Then, once I stopped working and I was home mornings, it was a lovely hour for me to have him watching television. That was absolutely a relief for me, to have that time. That was definitely how I saw it. I mean, it was good there were numbers and all those other things there, too . . . [laughing] but . . ."

While some mothers first set their children before the television primarily for the child's benefit, the majority of parents began using television in an open quest for relief. They look forward to those hours of peace so eagerly that sometimes they actually push the child into watching.

The mother of Ian, age 6, and Emma, age 4, recalls such a beginning:

"Ian first started watching television when he was two but he didn't get really addicted until he was three. At first many of the programs frightened him. Even 'Sesame Street' was too violent for him and he refused to watch it. But he was willing to watch 'Captain Kangaroo' and I guess I did encourage him to watch it. I loathed the mornings and it was a way to allow myself some time to feed the baby and to be quiet myself while he watched 'Captain.' I couldn't resist doing it."

Ian's mother was as unlikely to spurn the advantages offered her by television as she was to forgo the services of her washing machine and choose to scrub her laundry against the rocks at the nearest stream. And yet there was a price to pay, a price she didn't foresee when she enjoyed her peace and quiet: today Ian would rather watch television than do anything else.

As parents depend more and more on television until they find they cannot manage without it, television slowly infiltrates family life. One day they make the disturbing discovery that they have lost control over their child's television viewing.

Helen S., a part-time musician and mother, began using television as a handy child sedative while she prepared dinner. She describes the evolution of a serious television problem:

"There was a time when Kitty and John were both little, about two and three, when they watched nothing but 'Mr. Rogers.' Our whole dinner schedule was geared to that program, and I'd have dinner ready for them exactly at five-thirty when 'Rogers' was over. That was a nice useful time to have them salted away watching TV. I was the one who turned on the set at that time, and I didn't turn it on any other time. But that program was very convenient.

"Then there was a time when they watched 'Sesame Street' and 'Mr. Rogers.' That didn't seem too much television to me. But pretty soon a time came when 'Mr. Rogers' became too tame for John. When he was four he discovered 'Batman.' So now there was 'Sesame Street' and 'Batman.' And sometimes 'Underdog,' which both of them liked a lot. And then they developed a great fondness for 'The Flintstones.' I don't know where they got interested in all those other programs, maybe from baby-sitters, who always let them watch TV.

"Now I began to feel a bit uneasy about television. You see, I had been in such complete control at first.

But then, slowly, all these other programs infiltrated, and they seemed to want to watch so many things! So I decided to limit the time they spent watching instead of worrying too much about what programs they watched, since they seemed to like some programs so much.

"But what began to bother me was that John often refused to go out and ride his bike in the afternoon because he preferred to stay at home and watch TV. Well, I fought that tooth and nail! I'd explode and have a tantrum and say, 'We're not going to watch *any* television if it has that sort of a hold on you!' I'd make a scene about it and declare that we were going to have some new rules about television! But those never lasted very long. Also, I talked to the school psychologist about the television problem and she told me not to worry, that if John wanted to watch two or three hours of television, it was probably the best thing for him to do. Well, that went against all my instincts, but it was the easiest thing to do, to just let him watch.

"When they were six and seven they discovered the Saturday morning cartoons. They adored them and would watch them all morning. I can't deny that this was great for us, because we'd be able to lie in bed nice and late while they watched their programs.

"Then last year they discovered 'Jeannie.' [Groan.] The combined message of 'Jeannie' and 'The Flintstones' is so sexist that it makes me furious. But the school psychologist assured me that TV is just TV and that kids know it isn't real.

"Last year our pattern was a terrible one. 'Jeannie' was on from five-thirty to six-thirty, but our dinnertime was six o'clock. I'd tell the kids that if they insisted on watching 'Jeannie' they'd have to turn it off when dinner was ready. They'd say, 'Yeah, sure, we'll turn it off.' Then I'd come and warn them that dinner would be ready in five minutes. Then I'd come in and tell them to turn it off at the next commercial. Of course, they didn't turn it off. I'd always have to come in and turn it off and they'd be very angry about this. They'd say, 'I hate you,' and come into dinner shoving and kicking each other, angry and pouty, very, very angry. So dinnertime would be very unpleasant for all of us.

"They'd stay grumpy for the whole meal. It was the worst time of the day, really! And this went on all year. Every once in a while I'd get fed up and make threats like 'We won't watch TV anymore if this is what happens when you watch!' I don't think I ever made good on those fancy threats."

At this point in the narrative the mother stopped and said to the interviewer in a changed voice, "This is really a terrible saga, isn't it?"

Television and the Baby-sitter

What emerges from talks with parents about their children's television watching is a picture of parents' steady loss of control as they gradually withdraw from an active role in their children's upbringing. And as the parents grow less powerful, they discover themselves less and less capable of coping with their strong but undisciplined, grumpy, threatening children. Common sense suggests that without television, parents would have been unable to survive life under such circumstances; they would have been *forced* to socialize their children more persistently, *forced* to work a little harder at making them speak more agreeably or behave more considerately. But television, as the mothers' testimonies indicate, abolishes the need to establish those sorts of disciplines. There is no longer the impetus to ensure the sort of behavior that would allow a mother to cook dinner or talk on the telephone or assert herself as a parent in any way without being eaten alive, in a manner of speaking, by her children.

The poor socialization of children today has surely contributed to the exodus of mothers from the home. Of course, the Women's Liberation movement has played a major role in leading mothers away from a life of child care and domestic responsibilities. But it does not seem unlikely that the increased willfulness, demandingness, and disagreeableness of undisciplined children make a life of staying home seem less appealing than the drabbest, most routine office job so many women choose in exchange.

And television may be involved in the parental flight from children in yet another fashion. For in spite of the fact that parents seek to escape their children because they have brought them up to be difficult to live with, they nevertheless continue to love them as much as parents have ever loved their children. They know that a nurse-maid or baby-sitter is an inadequate substitute for a loving parent, and this makes them feel guilty. Moreover, their guilt and anxiety are compounded with fears concerning the treatment the child might be receiving in their absence: If the parents themselves are leaving home because the child is so difficult or disagreeable or whatever, *and they love the child,* to what state will the child drive the substitute parent? How will she cope? Might she not be driven to *lay hands on him?*

Such fears might ordinarily bring parents to stay at home and face the music—perhaps going so far as to work at training and disciplining their unruly children—but once again, television comes to the rescue. The parental burden of guilt and anxiety is considerably relieved by the knowledge that in their absence the child can spend his time sitting peacefully in front of the television set instead of driving the baby-sitter up the wall. Now the parents can leave with an easy mind. Parents often aver that baby-sitters *insist* on using television, that they could never even *get* a baby-sitter if they had no television set (there is some truth to this), and that their children's over-use of television is a result of the baby-sitter's reliance on television to make her life easier. But parents rarely admit that their own peace of mind *depends* upon the knowledge that their children are temporarily socialized and civilized, in their absence, by the television set.

"When I have a baby-sitter," says a mother who

normally limits her children's viewing time to an hour a day, "and I realize that the sitter has to control them, then I let them watch the TV whenever they want. One time I came home and realized that the kids had been watching TV from about two to eight. But I don't know if the sitter would have managed without TV."

14

Out of Control

"When I think about television now I feel like the person who always thought she was a moderate drinker and then one day sat down and added up her alcohol consumption and discovered she was a drunk! I started out with the attitude that the educational channel was the only one I'd let the kids watch. But all of a sudden, it started sneaking up on us. First it was 'Batman.' Then it was 'Batman' and 'Superman.' Then it was 'Batman,' 'Superman,' and 'The Lone Ranger.' And then they wanted to watch 'Star Trek,' too! By the end of a few weeks I thought, My God! What in the world's going on here?" relates a mother of three children.

Most of the problems parents face with television are not directly related to television itself, but to its control. It was this realization that prompted a newspaper reader responding to one of the periodic *Children's-television-is-terrible-what-shall-we-do* articles to suggest peevishly: "There is an immediate remedy available that does not seem to have occurred to them—turn off the set."[1]

And yet that is precisely what American parents cannot seem to do.

Real Conviction

A well-known child psychiatrist and author suggests that parents are deceiving themselves when they say they cannot control television, that it is "too much of a hassle" or "not worth the agony." She believes that for a number of reasons they'd don't really *want* to control their children's viewing.

"When parents tell me that they *can't* make a child do this or that, it's very easy to demonstrate that they haven't tried," the psychiatrist reports. "I'll ask them, 'Do you allow your three-year-old to walk around with a sharp knife? Do you allow her to cross the street by herself?' They'll immediately describe how they keep their child from running into the street or playing with sharp objects. So I say that obviously the child gets the message when they feel firmly about something. What's the difference, I ask them, about this particular thing that they say they can't control? They'll answer, 'Well, it's not so important,' or 'It's only a matter of my convenience.' Obviously they haven't given the child the message that they mean it, because within themselves they *don't really feel it firmly*. If parents want to control their children's television watching they have to make it clear that it's as important as not playing with sharp knives or running into a busy street."

Many of the difficulties parents encounter in controlling their children's television watching are compounded by a lack of certainty about what role they wish television to play in their family life, and a basic ambivalence about television:

"When they say they want to watch TV and it's a nice sunny day, I get really mad at them," says one mother of two small children. "I'll tell them that I'll go out to the park and play soccer with them and they'll say no, they'd rather watch a TV program. Well, it's terribly galling when that happens, but what I do all depends on my mood, because I'm very ambivalent about it. So sometimes I'll tell them, 'I think you're very stupid to stay indoors on a beautiful day, but that's your own decision,' and then other times I'll just slam it off and scream and march everybody out of the house."

Another mother describes similar feelings:

"I've always been in conflict with myself about television. The kids keep begging to watch, 'Oh Mom, please!' even when there's something better to do, and

I want to say, 'Absolutely not! I'm throwing it out the window!' But I don't really want to make it an issue. I don't want it to become a great big thing that we fight over all the time. So I've been very inconsistent about it, trying very hard to get them into other routines because I don't want to fight with them about it. Some days I feel that I have to fight, and other days . . . I just don't. Which I guess is not very good for them, but I'm so conflicted about it."

A mother of a five-year-old and a six-year-old gives evidence that *real conviction* is a basic requirement for successful control:

"One day I got fed up with the children watching TV in the morning before school. Our morning scene was pathetic. The kids would be fixed in front of the television set and want to eat their breakfast there, hardly able to move their arms or legs to get their clothes on. They looked like little mummies.

"Well, I'd been complaining about morning television for a long time, turning it off sporadically, yelling at them to get dressed, fussing about it—but not very consistently. Nothing really worked. I just thought it was hopeless to control their television watching at all, especially since I *do* use the set in the evenings to give me a rest from them. Doesn't everyone, though?

"Well, this time I absolutely decided we couldn't live like this and morning television watching had to stop. And as usual when I deliver an ultimatum with real conviction, it worked! That's the most exciting thing I've learned as a mother. If I say, 'I really think you'd better not,' then it never works. Or if I haven't made up my mind that this is absolutely the only way to deal with something, then it's reflected in the static I get back from the kids.

"But it only took a couple of days and the morning TV problem was eliminated. Just gone. The kids knew I meant it. And I guess *I* knew I meant it, too. Maybe that was even more important."

The Diminishing Authority of the Family

It is not only parents' secret reliance on television that explains their failure to control it, but also a loss of confidence in their own beliefs and in their abilities to act on them successfully.

The diminishing authority of the family in general has undoubtedly made it more difficult for parents to deal with the television problem. As the government, the schools, the medical profession, and other outside institutions have made inroads into the family's hegemony, parents have grown more dependent upon these institutions and less confident in their own abilities to raise children according to their own ideas and principles. Parents are less likely to rely on common sense and their private assessment of what is right or wrong when confronted with a problem such as how to limit their children's television viewing; they tend to wait for the government or the school or at least the child experts to tell them what to do.

Unfortunately for them, little real help has been forthcoming from any of these sources. The government's periodic efforts to assess the effects of television on children have dealt exclusively with program content. No efforts have been made to investigate parents' *use* of the television medium, or the effects of television availability upon child rearing or family life. No help is offered to parents struggling to control television in their daily lives.

Nor has the medical profession rewarded parents for their trusting dependence on them in matters of child rearing by providing guidance for their television problems. Parents accustomed to learning from their pediatricians how to deal with their children's temper tantrums, thumb sucking, and other behavior problems rarely receive advice about the use and abuse of television. In spite of the fact that television viewing may be their young patients' most time-consuming daily experience, doctors generally ignore the subject in their annual or semiannual consultations with mothers. An informal survey of pediatricians suggests that few if any doctors volunteer information to parents about the quantity of television viewing suitable to a young child's development. In most cases pediatricians seem to have no particular opinions on the subject besides the pragmatic observation that "Mothers need to use the set to get through the day." And yet the Hippocratic Oath adjures the doctor to "follow that method of treatment which I consider for the benefit of my patients"—not his patients' mothers.

The Education Establishment, rather than providing any sensible guidelines about television use, almost universally compounds family television problems by assigning programs for children to watch at home and by adopting a "with-it," television-centered approach in their teaching programs. Granted, teachers tend to assign "worthwhile" programs as home-viewing assignments; nevertheless these assignments frequently increase children's normal watching load. By assigning television programs, moreover, teachers are subtly reinforcing parents' fatalistic attitudes toward their children's television viewing: since they're going to watch a great deal of television anyway, they might as well be forced to watch something good.

Indeed, the schools' habit of assigning programs for homework frequently deters parents with serious television problems from taking the only step that might restore balance in their family life: getting rid of the television set entirely. "We can't manage without television," such parents say. "The children *have* to watch certain programs assigned at school." While such an answer might be a rationalization, reflecting an unwillingness to "unhook" themselves from television, nevertheless it is clear that the schools' generally acquiescent or enthusiastic attitude toward television does not offer parents the sort of help they badly need.

A mother of three children who is anxious about the number of hours her children spend watching television and yet who cannot seem to set limits casts some light upon the crisis of confidence that afflicts American parents today:

"What's wrong with me is that I don't know what's right and what's wrong and neither do my children. Now *my* mother, to this day, believes in right and wrong, and she believes she *knows* what's right and what's wrong. But I absolutely don't. Outside of a very few moral issues, I don't know what's right or wrong about a lot of things. And the TV brings that to a head."

Parents respond with almost pathetic gratitude to any help offered by powerful outside institutions. When a well-known nursery school in New York City sent a letter to its entire parent body advising them to limit their children's viewing time to a maximum of one hour each day, the step was greeted with almost ecstatic enthusiasm.

"That letter gave me the final push into curtailing television," says one mother.

"I was under heavy pressure," relates another mother, who described her three-year-old son's campaign to watch "Planet of the Apes," "Lost in Space," and other popular cartoons instead of his daily diet of "Mr. Rogers' Neighborhood," "so when the letter arrived I was relieved to tell him the school didn't want him to watch."[2]

According to the head of the school, some parents used the letter itself to stop their children from watching, saying, "See, here is a letter from the school saying too much TV is bad," even though the children are too young to actually read it.

"Parents feel guilty about their use of television," she explains. "They feel that somehow they oughtn't to be doing this. We hope that by taking a position on this issue the school will give parents that extra little push. We hope they will finally decide to do something about it."

A teacher at the school and a member of the committee that drafted the anti-television letter does not condemn those parents who needed a letter from school to find the courage to control television:

"I'm sympathetic to the parents' plight and I've soft-

ened incredibly since I've had children of my own,"
she allows. "I feel that parents are often doing the best
they can but they don't quite know what to do. They're
bullied by their kids, afraid to stand up to them, and
then they get into patterns that are hard to break. If
those parents have the help of someone with authority
so they can say, 'Look, the school tells you to turn
off the television set,' that's great. It might be better if
they could trust their own instincts and use their own
authority. But if the same end is served this way, I
can't help but feel that the means are worthwhile."

This relief at not having to lay down the law
themselves reflects the particular difficulty latter-day
parents have in saying "no" to their children. A child
psychiatrist considers the possible sources of parents'
fearful permissiveness:

"I don't tell people what they should or shouldn't do.
But I find among so many parents, not only of patients
but of children I meet in schools, a lot of conflict about
being able to raise their children according to their own
lights. There's so much input from television and books
and articles. But more important, they seem to be fearful of getting angry at their own children, fearful of
telling them to turn the television set off. These parents
feel that a child has to do what he likes. But in fact they
are fearful of having a direct and personal relationship
with their children. I work with parents to help them
understand their fears and to understand their children's needs. And when they begin to understand,
they stop having doubts about turning the television
set off. When parents get to feel a connection of
some kind with their children, they invariably begin to
turn the television set off. Sometimes they even get rid
of it."

A Pursuit of Democracy

A misplaced pursuit of democracy, a particularly
American failing, may help to explain why some parents have such difficulties controlling television. These
parents believe that it is somehow *undemocratic*

to restrict a child's television watching. Parents are reinforced in this belief by a number of writers who purport to advise them. The author of a book on children and television writes that imposing strict rules about television use "smacks of dictatorship in the home, not democracy," and warns parents that "flat fiats handed down make for openly rebellious or overly docile individuals."[3] Thus the fear of being undemocratic ("un-American") allows parents to shunt the blame for the results of their ineffective child rearing onto the child himslf.

A mother admits:

"I know it sounds weak, but I just hate to be the one to be constantly disappointing people, regulating them, stopping them from doing something they enjoy. I don't like to be the heavy in the family. I'd rather we were all on an equal footing. That's why I have so much trouble getting the kids to watch less television, even though I see it's not good for them to watch so much."

An English mother says:

"The peculiar thing about American mothers is that they feel uncomfortable about many of the things their children do, but they won't do anything about it. They'll let them do anything. They're afraid of an authoritarian setup; that would be un-American. They don't like their children watching television for so many hours, so they set up a family conference and discuss setting up rules and so on. But the children end up watching just as much television."

Related to parents' belief that democratic principles must prevail in child rearing, even with preschool children, is the particularly modern devaluation of parents' rights that has accompanied the acceptance of a more child-centered philosophy of raising children. This factor, too, serves to keep the parental hand from pushing the "off" button.

"When my kids are being awful and rude while I'm talking on the phone, instead of disciplining them there's a part of me that says, 'Yes, I'm on the phone too long,' " reports a harried young mother whose sympathy and understanding of her children's wants and needs have dimmed her awareness of her own rights. She cannot say "no" to her children because she has lost her perspective, seeing life exclusively from their point of view. Such a mother will not turn off the television set when the child wishes to watch, even though she feels that too much watching may have detrimental effects, because the child's desires take precedence over her own in most daily confrontations.

A mother of two children aged 8 and 4 reveals a similar inability to assert her feelings and take action about television:

"I wish I had the strength not to let my kids watch. I get home at five-thirty and make dinner—my husband comes home at six o'clock. So from five-thirty until seven or seven-thirty, the kids watch television. And there's the most horrible garbage on at those hours. Things I can't stand like 'The Flintstones.'

"I just don't have the strength to make them turn it off. And these children have an almost unlimited supply of toys. But with the TV, they never touch a lot of them. Still, when I *do* turn the TV off, they go in and play with their toys."

"Do As I Say, Not As I Do"

Frequently the parents' own viewing habits nullify their attempts to reduce their children's dependence on television. Parents who themselves have come to depend on television for amusement, relaxation, or escape find it hard to set limits on their own children's viewing. It makes them feel hypocritical to set up a "do as I say, not as I do" policy in their household, and their canny children will be quick to take advantage of their parents' insecurity.

A mother describes this dilemma:

"I try to limit the kids' TV watching, but Alfred likes to watch quite a bit. Limiting the kids means he'd have to limit himself, and he doesn't really want to do that."

A New York mother relates:

"When the kids were younger, up until the youngest was about eight, I was really terribly worried about their television watching. There were times when I was tempted to just throw the set out. But I didn't because I myself like to watch the movies and Carol Burnett. . . ."

Another mother notes:

"I'd probably miss it more than the kids. And feeling like that makes it very hard for me to say, 'No, you can't watch TV. It's not good for you.' Just as I can't say with any real conviction, 'Peter, it's bad to suck your thumb,' when I smoke!"

A Primitive Pleasure

Since it appears that many of the difficulties parents face in controlling television are related to modern child-rearing trends and sociological tendencies—permissiveness, the diminishing authority of the family, the growth of the suburbs, and so on—it might seem that had television existed a century ago, parents then, with their strong family structure and firm authoritarian ways, would have been able to keep it in hand. But perhaps even they would have succumbed. There is something unique about the hold television has upon children, regardless of the sociological or methodological context.

It is the parents' intuitive understanding of the depth of the child's involvement with television, an understanding partly informed by their observations of the intensity of his viewing behavior and partly by the extent of his grief when television is denied, that ultimately keeps them from turning off their sets and allows them to observe helplessly as their family life becomes increasingly dominated by television.

For television is not a light, casual affair for the young child. It is a pleasure mysteriously bound up with some of the child's most primitive gratifications. An indication of the special position television viewing holds in the young child's pleasure hierarchy is the frequency with which it is linked with basic oral and anal gratifications by psychiatrists, psychologists, and (in their use of it) parents themselves.

Many parents make observations similar to this:

"When Eric watches he uses his quilt—that's the only time he sucks his thumb. Not always, but usually. The only other time he uses his quilt is in bed."

A child therapist reports:

"When I tell a parent to cut out television from a child's life because it is clearly having a detrimental effect, I often meet the same reaction that I do when I tell parents to take their five-year-old out of diapers and insist on his using the toilet, or to take the bottle away from a four-year-old. The mother says, 'That's ridiculous. He's scared of the toilet. He'll never do it.' Or, 'That's impossible. He loves his bottle too much.' Well, I've had the same reaction from parents when I bring up television. They're terrified. It just seems too *terrible* a deprivation to turn off the television set entirely. When they feel ready to take the chance and try my advice, they are always astonished at how easy it was. The only difference is that they don't slip back with the diapers and the bottle. But they do slip back with the television set."

A psychoanalyst notes:

"Parents don't like their kids watching television because it's so entrancing and captivating that it falls into the category of those forbidden, mildly damaging, and enjoyable experiences like masturbation. They don't like to see their kid tune out, sitting in the corner and playing with himself. And just so, they don't like to see him sitting in the corner looking at the google-box for hours on end. It's too pleasurable."

Just as parents' understanding of the child's relationship to food leads them to use food as a threat, a punishment, an incentive, and a replacement for love, so, too, their understanding of the importance of television viewing in their child's life leads them to use television as an important punishment and reward.

Almost 50 percent of the children interviewed in a recent large survey reported that their parents used television deprivation as a form of punishment. In all likelihood it has become the most widely used punishment in America today.[4]

"I catch myself using TV for discipline, telling Jimmy that he can't watch if he doesn't behave, and my husband wisely tells me: don't do that. But it's tempting. It's like no dessert," admits a mother of a preschooler.

Television is also commonly used in toilet training today. Parents frequently place the potty in front of the television set to inspire the child to "perform." Some parents also hold out promises of special television programs as a reward for compliance with toilet-training requirements. Similarly, no-television is used as punishment for toilet-training lapses.

How can one explain the particular importance of the television experience in children's lives? What are the factors that help place television viewing on the same level of importance as eating, for instance, or other occupations that seem at first glance so much more basic than this mechanically-organized activity?

A part of the answer may lie in the importance of environmental stimulation, the sights, sounds, smells, and feels of the world around him, in the child's early experience. From the first days of life children respond selectively to sights and sounds. While the infant's life seems to center around eating and sleeping, the various stimuli that reach his eyes and ears are perhaps an equal necessity. Their importance is illustrated by experiments demonstrating that infants will inhibit their most crucial activity, sucking at the breast or bottle, when presented with something new to look at or listen to.[5]

Parents and others with intimate dealings with small children have a practical understanding of the importance of environmental stimulation. They know that a child can be distracted from physical pain or painful emotional situations such as separation from his mother by having a shiny bracelet dangled before him or a lively song sung to him. Sometimes the sight of a particular color acts to soothe a fussing baby; often taking

a crying baby to a window looking out on a busy
street has a quickly calming effect.

It might be postulated that the child has a need
for taking in sensory material, just as he has a need for
taking in food and receiving affection. Fulfilling this
need for sensory input, then, may be as pleasurable
for the child as eating and cuddling.

Perhaps television's unique concentration of perceptual pleasures in a single quantum of experience—
moving images, attractive and interesting sounds, combined with the repetitive nature of these stimuli on
the screen and augmented further by the cognitive
fascinations of recognizable human sounds and images
—provides a uniquely pleasurable experience. Whereas none of the single components of the television experience would rank anywhere near the basic, primitive pleasures of eating or eliminating in satisfaction
value, all of them together may afford an overpower-
ing gratification.

But surely another part of the answer to the question of why television takes on so great an importance
in children's lives lies in the fundamental human struggle between passivity and activity. This struggle is particularly strong during early childhood, when the
human being makes the transition from almost total
physiological and psychological dependence and passivity to self-propelled activity and independence.
Erich Fromm describes man's "craving to be freed
from the risks of responsibility, of freedom, of awareness; his longing for unconditional love, which is offered without any expectation of his loving response,"[6]
a craving and longing that underlies many of man's
activities and that tries to undermine his drive to
control his environment, to explore, to master, to give
rather than to merely receive love.

In his television experiences the child returns to that
comfortable, atavistic passivity that was once his right
and that he must now renounce if he is to become a
functioning member of society. It is only while he
watches television that he is freed of the risks of real

life. His progress in the direction of activity, of giving, of "doing," is impeded by his television involvement.

Small wonder, then, that parents find it so hard to stick to their guns when they decide to limit their children's television viewing. In their children's wails and lamentations, in their pleas and entreaties, in the endless bargains they try to strike ("Just let me watch this extra program today and then I won't watch *any* TV tomorrow"), parents hear the true note of desperation. Without an unwavering conviction that the particular pleasures provided by the television are not in the same life-enhancing category as the basic gratifications of life, that television viewing does not foster growth but rather prevents the child from acting in a way that would make him prosper, parents do not have the heart, quite simply, to turn the television set off.

A mother who decided to eliminate television entirely two years ago thinks back to her former struggles with television control:

"I guess like most mothers I just hated to spoil their pleasure, even though I felt they were getting pleasure out of something that was not strictly worthwhile. It just seemed hard and mean to deprive them of their programs when they wanted to watch *so much.* Now that we don't have a set it seems different. Somehow I don't feel that they're being deprived. On the contrary, I get a feeling that the TV was actually depriving them of doing a lot of good things they do now. . . ."

The "Tired-Child Syndrome"

The extent of parents' dependence on television and their inability to control their children's television viewing is illustrated in the episode of the "Tired-Child Syndrome," as reported in *The New York Times.*[7]

Pediatricians at two air force hospitals were puzzled by the incidence of a syndrome of anxiety symptoms—chronic fatigue, loss of appetite, headache, and vomiting—in a group of 30 children whose parents had brought them in for diagnosis. When the doctors discovered that the children were spending three to six hours watching television daily, and six to ten hours on weekends, they began to suspect excessive television viewing might have something to do with the children's condition and instructed the parents to cut it out entirely.

The effects were dramatic in the 12 children whose parents followed the instructions fully: the symptoms vanished within two to three weeks. However, the parents of the other 18 children were unable to comply and allowed up to two hours of viewing a day, in spite of the fact that the doctor had ordered them to cut out television entirely. Nevertheless, with a significant reduction in their daily viewing even these children were free of symptoms in three to six weeks.

A later follow-up revealed a dismaying situation: of the 26 children whose cases were followed for several months, only 9 remained free of symptoms; all of them were still restricted in their viewing. Of the rest, restrictions had been lifted entirely for 13 children and 11 of these were again suffering severe symptoms. Four others were allowed limited viewing and had limited disorders.

From the scientific point of view it is difficult to prove that television viewing directly caused the symptoms of the "tired-child syndrome." Perhaps the new activities replacing television in the lives of those children whose viewing had been restricted—the increase in playing, talking, running around, and generally behaving like children—helped bring about the cure.

The most significant thing about this episode may be the fact that more than two-thirds of the parents of the children involved were unable to stick to the restriction, even though it had been prescribed as a treatment by their pediatrician and even though their children's symptoms returned as soon as they relented.

A further indication of these parents' enslavement to television is seen in a chilling fact: chlorpromazine, a strong sedative, had been prescribed for some of the children to aid them during the early days of treatment. Some of the parents who had trouble restricting their children's television viewing asked for *further* sedation of their children, preferring that alternative to the inconvenience of life without television.

15

Controlling Television

Some parents engage in a continuous, and largely un-successful, struggle to control television. Others find it too difficult to maintain a rich and various family life with a television set in the home and choose to live without it altogether.

A certain number of families, however, manage to coexist in relative peace with their television set and suffer few of the control problems that seem to beset most American parents.

How do these parents succeed when so many others flounder and fail? Sometimes success lies in their ability to be strict about television, to set up firm and non-negotiable rules about viewing. In other cases parents are helped by certain "natural" forms of control.

Firm Rules

The difficulties of controlling children's television viewing—the powerful attractions of the television experience, the diminishing authority of the family, the lack of support from schools and other institutions, the pressure from peers—all conspire to sap parents' confidence and make it difficult for them to deny their children the gratifications of television, to set firm rules and stick with them. But some parents manage to dredge up the strength to be strict, and as a result, television ceases to be a problem.

A child psychoanalyst who does not advise parents one way or the other about their television problems, believing that they must ultimately bring up their children "according to their own lights," has no television problems within his own family. The father of four children, he reports that they rarely watch television:

"Our kids are crippled as far as television is concerned. We don't *discourage* television watching—we simply turn the set off and tell them there are better things to do."

A number of families solve their television-control problems by a no-television-during-the-school-week rule, which becomes so accepted a part of family life that they live a virtually television-free existence five days a week, enjoying leisurely, conversation-filled meals and a pace of life dominated by their own human needs. The children do their homework without the pressure of television programs to make them hurry to get through. On weekends they enjoy television as other families do, but without the nagging anxiety that it is eating away at their family life and family relationships.

There are no statistics available to show how many families cut off television on school days, but it is interesting to note that in 1969, when he was vice president in charge of children's programming at CBS, Mike Dann informed an interviewer "that as his own children were growing up he did not permit them to view programs during the week . . . they were compelled to do something more intellectually alive."[1]

Yet other families set a strict daily time limit of no more than one hour a day on their children's viewing. This works to de-televisionize family life considerably, although not as effectively as a real hiatus from television. Parents sometimes are persuaded by their children to set a time limit of *more* than an hour a day. Indeed, some families feel that they have asserted the proper parental firmness in restricting their children to as much as three hours a day. Perhaps compared to seven hours of television viewing daily, a diet of three hours is an improvement for a child; nevertheless such a liberal limit does not make enough of a difference in a family's life style—television, television talk, television plans continue to dominate. A mother who has limited her children's daily viewing to two hours describes her continuing dissatisfaction with television's effects on her family life:

"What concerns me so much is not how to control television, because we've set up some rules and the kids have to observe them. But what I can't stop them from doing is *talking* about television. I wish I could play you back an average conversation that goes on at our dinner table. The kids talk about nothing but what went on in this program and that program. Who did what to whom, who said what, and then what happened. Sometimes my husband and I will tell them to stop, that we don't want to hear any more about television programs. What happened in school today? We'll ask. So there's a brief interlude and they'll quickly tell us something about school and then right back to the TV, which actor played what part, and on and on and on."

Another family (who ultimately got rid of their television set permanently) dealt with a similar problem by trying to set rules about family conversations rather than setting limits on television watching:

"So much of Alexander's dinnertime conversations had to do with television—either he'd repeat jingles from commercials or else he'd relate incidents from programs at great length about what one caveman did to another caveman and the like—that we tried to set up a rating system for which topics were suitable for conversation and which were not. We called the suitable topics GC—General Conversation. Television talk was definitely *not* GC. I started this system because I had a dismal feeling that we never had a chance to really talk to each other, to find out what we thought about things, or felt—what *we* were like. Conversations were just extensions of watching television."

Some families' control problems are compounded by a lack of agreement between the parents themselves about the *need* to control television.

A father of a five-year-old describes such a situation:

"We limit Peter's television time to an hour a day,

and things are working out fine now. But we used to get into the most tremendous fights with Peter about television. We had a lot of trouble saying no about TV because he'd throw a real fit, an absolute tantrum, and that scared us, or at least me. I didn't really think television was so bad; I didn't think it was worth the struggle, since he wanted to watch so badly. But now the television stays off even if he throws a fit. An hour a day, that's the rule, and we stick to it. Actually he doesn't bother throwing a fit anymore. He knows the rule's there. But it took us several years to establish it. [Laughs.] Several years for my wife and me to agree enough to establish it. Once it was established, Peter caught on quickly. But when my wife and I were not completely in agreement about television, he saw right away that this was a great opportunity to bug us, to drive a wedge between us. He saw how easily he could get us going with the whole television thing."

A mother notes:

"I'm trying to kick the habit for my children but it's too hard. They want to see this and they want to see that and then there's all the specials they have to see because their friends are going to be watching. I try to be firm, but their father is not as disgusted with the whole children's television scene as I am, and so he tells them yes."

Indoctrinating against Television

In the struggle to control television certain parents discover that their own negative attitudes toward television can work effectively to reduce their children's interest in it. Often, indeed, the feeling that they have *explained* their feelings convincingly helps normally permissive parents feel better about enforcing rules about television.

"I've been telling the children my feelings about television for a long time," says a mother of two young boys, "and I think they've been indoctrinated. I explain that it's better to *do* than to just watch. When we're at a toy store I point out certain toys that I call television-type toys, toys you wind up and they do things while you just sit there, and I really put down that kind of toy. We talk about toys that you can have some sort of an effect on, like ropes and strings and balls, toys where you can do something and the toy can become anything in the world. They understand how I feel, and while wind-up toys and television have attractions for them, as passive entertainments often do (and of course, they do watch occasionally), they seem to have developed a certain amount of resistance to them."

The father of a six-year-old describes an incident that proved useful in resolving a television problem:

"At one point our son was very sad after watching 'Six Million Dollar Man' with me because he said there was something he wanted to *tell* me during the program but he didn't because he was afraid he might miss something on the program. I told him, 'You see what television is doing to you? You wanted to talk to me about something important and television wouldn't let you. It's taking us apart, at least a little bit. We're a family and we want to talk to each other, but television keeps us from talking.' It really sank in, believe it or not. He doesn't seem to be as eager to watch anymore. Our family relationships are very serious and very sacred to us and to our children. I just tried to put it to him in this way and it worked."

A Denver mother who limits her children's viewing to two hours *a week,* weekends only, reports:

"There's a great difference in the children's feeling about TV. It's not the central part of their life anymore. They can kind of take it or leave it. But they notice that other kids watch a lot of TV and they kind of look down their noses on kids who depend on it. [Laughs.] A little snob appeal! They realize that other kids have to depend on TV for their entertainment while they don't have to. Of course we've talked to them pretty heavily about this. They're proud that they can actually sit down and entertain themselves, very much so."

A writer advises parents not to "bad-mouth" television, "for if children then spot their mother and father watching TV, they will lose their respect for them."[2] It undoubtedly is far easier to control children's television viewing if the parents do not spend much time watching television while the children are awake. Still there is no reason why parents who set strict rules about their children's television time should have to be furtive about the programs they want to watch themselves. Their own lives, after all, are different in many ways from the lives of their young children: they work, they have adult responsibilities, and they engage in a number of adult activities they would not dream of including their children in. Television viewing is but one of these adult activities.

Natural Control

For parents who lack the reserves of strength necessary to set rules and stick to them in spite of wheedling, whining, pleading, or most painful of all, angry cries of "I hate you!" there are certain "natural" methods of television control that do not require discipline or any extensive change in child-rearing style. These have to do with physical factors concerning the sound and placement of the set itself, and often allow parents who cannot say "no" in an old-fashioned and perhaps undemocratic way to live in relative peace with their television sets.

Parental sensitivity to sound is one such factor that often acts as a natural limit. Different mothers and fathers have mentioned:

"Somehow I can't stand the sound of it, especially the manic sound of cartoons and ball games. It drives me crazy and I go and turn it off."

"I'm very aware of sounds, and noise really bothers me. The continual *something* talking over there in the corner, adding to the general din, is quite intolerable to me. That's probably the only reason I'm strict about television because I'm not strict about anything else."

"When we listen to television, its always on at a

lower level than anywhere else I know. Everybody else's kids come to our house and turn up the volume. But I can't stand that. But because I don't like the noise, I don't think the kids get quite as zonked out by TV when it's on very quietly. It doesn't seem to blow their minds quite as much."

The set itself, its condition and location in the house, often serves as a natural limit to a family's television viewing.

"I don't like watching television much," says an eight-year-old boy who watches little television, "because we have a terrible television set. It keeps messing up and either the sound is bad or the picture or both. Worst of all we sometimes get a double picture. Grandma's set is also pretty bad."

In some families the decision to live with a poor television set is made quite deliberately.

"We inherited an old set," reports an English teacher and father of two young children. "The reception was terrible. My wife thought that perhaps we ought to have it fixed, or buy a better set, but I persuaded her to continue with the old set. We could still see a program if we wanted to, but it wasn't easily accessible. Most of all it made the whole experience less enticing for us, and we needed that. We all tended to do a lot of watching when we had a good set."

In deciding *where* to locate the television set, many families consider the problem of control and the effects of television on family unity:

"Our set is in the living room because we feel it's less likely to separate the family there. It also helps cut down on the kids' viewing because when we have company the kids can't watch. That's all there is to it, and they accept that better than if we tried to make rules about when they can watch and when they can't."

Some families go even further in their efforts to find a way to limit their children's television viewing:

"We used to have our television upstairs in the living room, but it was just too accessible and tempting there. We were having all sorts of problems with it and felt that the kids—all of us, really—were just watching too much. We didn't want to get rid of the set altogether, so we put it down in the basement. It's pretty dilapidated and unpleasant down there, not the sort of place you want to lie around all evening watching television."

Another family made a similar decision:

"We keep our set in the basement to have it out of the way. It's there because we don't like to talk over the TV, as happens at our friends' houses, or to have other people distracted by it and lose the thread of the conversation. Also, in the basement there's less of a temptation to just flick it on when you enter the house. You have to make a special trip down there to watch something."

Operating on the "out of sight, out of mind" principle, some families go so far as to put their television set in a closet after each use. The effort required each time the family wants to watch ensures a certain amount of selectivity. It also effectively prevents the children from overindulging in television when the parents are out, even though baby-sitters sometimes take the trouble of bringing the set out of the closet in order to watch their *own* programs.

A slightly less radical but nevertheless effective method is used by this New York family:

"One of the things that helps us not watch so much television is that we have a small black and white set and it's not stationary. It stands in a corner and it has to be especially put out on a table in order to watch. That makes watching a little inconvenient. The set's not right *there,* ready and waiting. In some homes I've noticed that the television set is so central that you can practically not do anything else but watch when it's on. But since ours is so small and you have to go to all the trouble of setting it up, we tend to use it only for special occasions."

A reverse example of natural control is the natural

decontrol that occurs when a television set is located in a child's own room. The principal of an elementary school states:

"Sometimes parents mention in the course of a conference that the kids have a set in their own room. I'll say, 'For heaven's sake why do you have to give your child his own television set? That decontrols the situation completely.' And their answer always is, 'Well, we don't want to have to hear their programs in the living room.' But when they don't hear the programs, they stop trying to cut down on television completely."

A rich social life may also serve as a natural limit to children's television viewing. A family with two children aged 10 and 8 who live in an ample apartment in New York find that the television set is infrequently used in spite of a permissive attitude toward it. The parents feel this is because there are always a number of extra children in the house, temporarily or semipermanently.

"I'm terrible about organizing the children's social lives," the mother reports, "but there's always an enormous amount of activity going on. We usually have one or two older kids living with us, daughters of friends who live out of town. Also we live on the way to Lucy's school and she almost always brings girls home with her, sometimes ten at a time! Jeremy usually brings home a couple of kids since his school is nearby, too. But he has a friend who lives upstairs, an only child, and that child watches television a great deal. Maybe there's a connection."

A psychiatrist agrees that the television problem depends on a family's social circumstances:

"The television problem is related to small families. Amusing small kids would be perfectly easy if you had four or five kids of various ages around at all times to amuse each other. The whole idea of a mother entertaining a small child is kind of crazy, anyway. It never happened prior to 1900."

A child therapist discusses her own need for an

extended family and relates such a need to the television problem:

"When you have children, then that small nuclear family life ought to come to an end. It's painful to end it. It's hard to have much less privacy. But I don't feel I can give my child all the attention that he deserves to have, that's good for him to have, that he needs to flourish. I need my husband's interest and activity, and I also need my sisters and my mother and so on. It provides relief for me, a change of scene, it eliminates that stuck feeling, it's great for the baby. Maybe this is the great underlying reason for television's powerful hold on parents—it's sitting in for the extended family. There aren't enough resources within a single family to give your children. Television fills a vacuum."

As Sarane Boocock writes, "The care of young children, an activity which requires full time availability but not full time attention and action, is most 'efficiently' carried out in a setting in which other activities are also being carried out."[3] Thus, in the past, the economic functioning of the home necessitated an organization in which a number of people were available to share in child care. In today's small family the lonely, isolated mother turns to the television set for the sort of service once provided by other family members, neighbors, and friends who were ever-present.

IV

NO TELEVISION

16

Before and After Experiments

One way to study the effects of regular television viewing on family life would be to compare a number of families who watch television regularly with a number of similar families who do not watch at all. However, since the overwhelming majority of American families fall into the category of television owners, there simply aren't enough no-television families for a well-matched comparison. Moreover, even if a sufficient number were found, the results of such an experiment would still be equivocal: there are too many subtle differences among individual families even when matched according to class, income, size, education, or whatever, and too many other possible variations in life styles besides the presence or absence of a television set.

A simpler experiment involves the before-after approach. Take a television-viewing family and eliminate television entirely for a period of time. Then examine the differences between its daily life with television and without. In such an experiment each family is compared only with itself; therefore the results are far more likely to reveal television's effects than those of a study comparing different families.

Three such before-after experiments are described here. The first falls into the category of an "experiment of nature" foisted on a family who moved into a mountain area with no television reception. The second involves a family that studied the effects of a two-week television blackout; the third concerns 15 families who turned off their sets for at least a month and noted the differences in their family life.

1. The Cable Vision Truck Never Came

"We are a family of four who lived for two and a half years without television," reports Mrs. Lee of Glenwood Springs, Colorado. "I am twenty-eight and a registered nurse and my husband is thirty-one and in the insurance business. Our daughter is now eight, and our sons are five and six.

"Before we moved to Vail because of my husband's work, we lived in Colorado Springs. The children were TV addicts even though I consciously tried to monitor what they watched and limit them somewhat. I was very concerned about their TV watching. I'd watch my daughter go into a trancelike state whenever the TV was turned on—it made no difference what she was viewing. The boys were generally much more active than their sister and at first seemed less keen on television. However, as time went on, they, too, seemed to become totally passive in front of the television set.

"In November, 1971, we moved to Vail—actually five miles east of Vail. Soon we learned that our house was beyond the reach of Cable Vision, and without the cable there was no reception at all. The mountains simply blocked all signals.

"At first we thought it was a temporary state of affairs and tried to fill our free time as best we could, always with the idea that television would be restored any day. We played our record collection until I was sick of every record. We talked about television a lot.

"Before long we began to realize that we'd probably never see that Cable Vision truck pull in to hook up our set. We became resigned to our fate. Then life began to settle down into a more normal pattern. We began to read books, not just magazine stories. We'd play with the children for over an hour at a time sometimes, and they'd play by themselves for increasing periods of time, too. We entertained other couples much more than we used to. I started some serious sewing and experimented with new recipes. There just seemed to be much more time in a day.

"Our daughter became quite good at entertaining herself by trying to read. She painted, drew pictures, modeled clay, wrote 'letters' to all the family and her playmates. Several times a week she helped me bake cookies and cupcakes. Daddy taught her to play a serious game of checkers before she was six. I read at least one story a day to her and to the boys. We had a book on children's crafts and hobbies and several times a week we'd set aside an afternoon to make or play something new. Also I kept a large box of Halloween costumes and old dresses that my daughter and her friends and even the little boys loved to play with and never seemed to tire of. They loved best playing store and school and hospital. Many, many broken legs, heads, and arms did I bandage with cloth from the special costume box! Of course there was outside play, but on many winter days we couldn't go out for more than a few minutes, and all the swings and playground equipment were buried under snow for several months.

"We did get to see some television during our Vail stay, however. Three or four times a year we'd go to visit Grandma, and we'd get to watch television. It was a real treat for all of us, just like going to the movies used to be before I ever saw television.

"Then after two and a half years without TV in Vail, we moved again, because of my husband's work. We swore we'd never get addicted again. But even though we may not watch TV to the extent of many families I know, still I'm afraid we're caught again. I use the TV as a baby-sitter maybe two hours every day. We're in an apartment complex with no play facilities and having the television is just too tempting sometimes.

"I try not to watch too much myself, but if I'm too tired to do anything else, I'll watch. Our daughter is addicted to the seven a.m. 'Lassie' reruns and 'The Lone Ranger.' If she starts watching an evening show, she has to watch it through to the end, even if she doesn't understand the story.

"My husband isn't home much because of his new business, but if he sits down in the living room at all, the TV has to be on. He hasn't played with the children at home since we've moved here. We have gone out as a family on picnics, jeep trips, and fishing, but at home there is no more family roughhousing, piggyback rides, et cetera. No more checkers, either."

2. Don Brawley's Experiment[1]

In 1972 Don Brawley, a young black policeman on the New York City force, began work at Brooklyn College in a special program for police officers. One of his courses that year was sociology, for which he was required to devise a simple research experiment. He decided to disconnect his television set for two weeks and observe the effects on his own family life.

Brawley got an A for his paper, parts of which are included below:

First, a few things should be known about my household. The annual income is $20,000 a year, the education level of the adults is one year of college. We live in a suburban area about 35 miles from the city limit. My family consists of myself, my wife, and two sons, aged five and six years old. My two sons, who share the same bedroom, have their television located there. My wife and myself have a television located in our bedroom.

As a prerequisite for this experiment, I charted the time in which each television was in use for the period of one week. The children's television was used for a total of 41 hours, which is approximately 6 hours each day, and my wife's television was used for a total of 18 hours. However, some consideration could be given to the time of year in which this experiment took place; it was in the month of April. I was on vacation for three weeks.

At the start of the actual experiment, I had to devise a way to put both televisions out of service. The first was the portable television, which belongs to the children. I removed the fuse from the rear. The second was a large color console, in which I found a main control for the horizontal hold in the rear of the set. By turning the button, I rendered the television useless.

The first day of the experiment showed no real effects of the loss of television from the household. My wife went about her daily routine and the children spent much of the day playing in the backyard. It was that night when I noticed the first effects of not having a television set working. It was now too dark to send the children out to play and my wife found it quite impossible to do her evening work with children in her way. This resulted in the children retiring early. This was a solution to the first problem but caused a greater one.

The very next day the children woke up at 6:30 in the morning. When the television is working, the children turn it on about 7 a.m. Each day the television would perform the duties of a baby-sitter from the time the children woke up until the time my wife got up from bed. The children constantly annoyed my wife until she got up and made breakfast. My oldest son was off from school because of the Easter holiday. What caused the major problem that day was the rain. By twelve o'clock my wife left the house to visit a neighbor and watch the stories that come on television each afternoon. As the day progressed, each member of the family became more and more annoyed over small things. Each day thereafter became more and more routine.

The children spent a great deal of time doing creative things that their mother planned for them each day, learning to write their alphabet, cutting out the letters and drawing on their blackboard. The puzzles came from out of the closet, and other toys that the children never had the particular interest to play with before soon took up much of their day. I could begin to see where the children spent more time doing things which would be of importance to them in their school work in the future.

The amount of time that my wife now spent actively with the children increased considerably. Also she now did a lot more tasks around the home. The closets that stored old clothes and other useless things were cleaned out. The guest room that had not been used for over three months got a thorough cleaning. She used to make her own clothes and sewed very well. With nothing to do in the evening, she started to sew again. By the middle of the second week of the experiment, she had completed a dress and started another one.

As a participant observer in the experiment, I found myself becoming completely bored at times. And like the rest of the family, I made certain changes in my daily activities. I also started to do those chores that somehow always got put aside until the next week. For the first time since I had been in school, I was completely caught up with all the reading for my courses.

After the long winter of not seeing most of the neighbors we began to visit different families who, during the winter months, we lost contact with.

During the experiment I noted a positive effect on our sex life. I attribute it to the early hours that we kept and the amount of rest we received each day. In the past we went to bed after the eleven o'clock news or one of us would watch the late show or some other show that would keep us apart.

The children seemed to fight among themselves more often. However, there is the possibility that it was noticed and paid more attention to because my wife and I were bothered by small things. At the same time the children became closer to us as we participated in doing things together. An average weekend at my house would consist of Saturday morning doing all the work around the house that was necessary and Saturday night taking the wife out. Sunday morning was Sunday School for the boys and church for the wife. In the afternoon, I would have some kind of activity with the boys. During the second week of the experiment, we went out three times in one week. As a family, we worked together on the lawn and preparing the garden for the summer; doing things the family had not done before as a unit.

At the end of the second week both televisions were operating. I wanted to once again compare the differences of having a television and not having one. All of the good things that had flourished because of the absence of a television set now disappeared. Everything reverted back to its old routine.

3. The Denver No-Television Experiment

In the spring of 1974 an article appeared on the television and radio page of the Sunday *Denver Post* inviting families with young children to volunteer for an informal experiment in which they would turn off their television sets entirely for a period of time no shorter than a month.[2]

Over a hundred responses expressing interest in the experiment were received. A number of letter writers, though intrigued, admitted that they *couldn't,* for one reason or another, actually eliminate television. Among their reasons:

"I'm afraid that if I gave up television the kids would take up a whole bunch more of my time—and I don't have time to spare."

"My husband doesn't share my opinion of television viewing. When he's home, he watches almost continually."

"If it weren't for 'Mr. Rogers' and 'Electric Company,' I'd never get dinner ready or the entrance steps vacuumed."

"My child has a broken leg and needs to watch television. Maybe I'll try it *next* summer."

Others explained that they had already eliminated television. (Interviews with some of these families appear later in this chapter.) Still others wished to volunteer, but had no small children in the house, or had children younger than 2. (Since the greatest use of television is made by parents of young children, and since family styles are often established when children are young, it had been decided to limit the experiment to families with at least one young child at home.)

Questionnaries about family background and television use, as well as suggestions for preparing children for the no-television period and for dealing with problems that might arise, were sent to twenty-five families. A diary was sent in which to record television use and behavior for a few weeks before the experiment and to note any changes that occurred during the no-television period.

Of the twenty-five families receiving questionnaires and diaries, fifteen actually completed the experiment and sent in their questionnaires and diaries. These families were interviewed in their homes at least once during their no-television periods, and once by phone a month or two after the experiment was over.

Why did these families volunteer for the experiment in the first place? A general tone of anxiety is heard in many of their answers to this question:

"My own TV watching has become too much. I use it as a substitute for everything."

"We rarely do things we mean to do—television is just too much of a habit."

"I'd like the children to do something other than watch TV. I'd like them to be aware of how much TV they watch and how many more exciting things there are to do."

"I'd like to eliminate some of the hassle connected with television in our family, and also to have the children explore other means of entertaining themselves."

"To help our family discover alternative forms of time structuring."

"I really have trouble communicating with my nine-year-old. He always has his nose in the television. Even the neighbors notice it. They'll say, 'Andy, it's time to go home for supper now,' and he'll sit there glued to the set. He watches about four or five hours a day and it really worries me."

How did the children whose parents volunteered for the no-television experiment react to the idea of temporary elimination of television from their homes?

In those families with preschool children the parents were surprised to find that the children hardly noticed the absence of television from their daily routine. Some school-age children were enthusiastic, at least at the start. A number, however, voiced anger and resentment at their parents for depriving them of television:

"When we presented the no-television experiment, as a 'we-are-doing-it' fact to our four children (aged ten, nine, eight, and five), their reaction was one of anger toward the lady who had suggested the experiment in the article. I found the article torn and crushed on the table the next day—I think it was a group effort."

"My children's reactions to the experiment jolted me. My ten-year-old son—probably the worst addict of us all—was all for it, named neighbors he thought would concur with the idea, and was intrigued with being part of a study about television. My nine-year-old daughter was horrified and indignant about the whole thought. My seven-year-old said, 'Okay, but can we get a piano instead of a TV?'"

"Michael (six and a half) was upset that he would miss the Saturday cartoons," reports one mother, "but I reminded him that he had seen nothing but reruns for the past couple of months. He admitted that was true and didn't object to the experiment after that."

Most of the families reported experiencing some difficulties during the first days of the experiment, some of them comparing that period to "withdrawal" from drugs or alcohol. In all cases the parents and children reported that as time went on, they missed television less and less:

"The first week was hard for all of us, especially the kids and me. They sort of hung around and didn't know what to do with themselves. I suggested reading, which we did a lot of, but still time was long sometimes. After the first week it began getting easier and easier for all of us. By the end of the first month we really didn't miss TV at all," wrote a mother whose family engaged in the no-television experiment for two months.

A nine-year-old boy told an interviewer, "Sometimes, the first few days after Dad unplugged the set I'd just go and look at it, even though it was off. I really missed watching. Then as the summer went on, I stopped thinking about TV so much."

"At the beginning the children kept asking to watch TV. They really seemed to miss it and we began to wonder whether the whole thing wasn't too hard on them. But gradually they found other things to do that we thought were a lot better than watching television."

During the "withdrawal" period a number of children reported feeling disoriented and "weird." "It just didn't seem like summer," said a ten-year-old girl. A nine-year-old told an interviewer, "I'd keep going to somebody's house and I wanted to know what day of the week it was. I always know what day it is from what programs are on."

Among the changes in family life noted by parents in their diaries were the following:

More interaction with adults

"Cathy had a girl friend over and they sat around with the adults in the evening, listening and joining in the conversation. We enjoyed that and realized that in the past the kids always watched TV when we had company."

A more peaceful atmosphere in the home

"I've enjoyed the quietness of life without TV. I was thinking that maybe after the experiment we ought to find another place for the set besides the family room."

"There seems to be so much more time. Perhaps part of it is that there isn't that frantic, hurrying sound of the TV always in the background."

"I would say that not having to adjust between watching TV and playing made for a more restful atmosphere in the home. I'd noticed that the 'coming out' of the television spell and adjusting to a play situation was often a lengthy process, full of antagonism between children."

A greater feeling of closeness as a family

"The children and I became closer because we did more things together."

"The family, I feel, is pulling together tighter as a result of no TV."

"The difference has been enormous. We feel we're a family again, united by common experiences and bonds. We discovered many things about each other during the experiment, hidden talents and interests."

"We did more things together as a family during the experiment. We wanted that and we got that."

More help by children in the household

"I used to let the kids watch TV after dinner because their favorite programs were on then and it seemed too mean to deprive them. Then I had to do the dishes alone. Now they have time to help. We do a lot of talking while doing dishes. It's a very comfortable sort of time when it's easy to talk—maybe the soapy water makes us all relax."

"Betty helped Dad with yard work and then helped him wash the truck."

"Both children cleaned their rooms more thoroughly than usual, and spent a lot of time alphabetizing the books in their bookcase and arranging the things on their desks."

More outdoor play

"In the past we couldn't get the kids outside if my husband held open the door and I booted them out. Now they're going out in all sorts of weather with no television to keep them inside."

"We noticed there's a lot more outdoor play, even when the weather isn't great."

Changes in bedtime and meals

"We found we were all going to bed much earlier."

"Dinners are longer now since the children don't leave to watch their programs."

"Mealtimes are given to general conversation, instead of arguments about how soon they could get up and watch TV."

Children play together more

"The children seem to deal with each other more without the TV. When there's nothing to do, they're likely to play with each other, really do things together."

"The girls are apt to play regular, organized games now that the TV is out. They played together before, but now they're more likely to play games with rules, board games. And the older one is more willing to play with the younger, whereas before it was easier to just watch TV and not take the extra trouble of explaining the rules of a game to a younger sister."

"Our children are playing together, real old-fashioned playing. The two middle children made up an entire musical today entitled 'Dolphins in the Desert.' "

"Now that the children have to depend on themselves and each other for entertainment, they're playing together a lot more."

More reading

"Although the children have always enjoyed reading,

we noticed a definite increase in the number of books read during the no-television period."

"Joey always reads a lot. The difference is that he'll start reading in the middle of the afternoon and read through the time to go to bed. He wouldn't have done that with the TV available."

Better relations between parents

"My husband misses the sports events, but I enjoy talking to him."

"Personally I find I can tolerate Saturday housework as a working mother a lot better when I don't see my husband loafing near the TV."

More activities

"There's a definite increase in activities on the part of the children."

"We have more time for games, crafts, model building, and reading."

"We did several alternate activities this summer: planted a large vegetable garden, various arts and crafts."

"When the kids had nothing to do, they went out and made a secret hideout—played there for many days."

"I did more sewing during the no-TV period than I've done in years."

Among the problems related to no television mentioned by parents and children:

Favorite programs

"I've missed not watching 'Masterpiece Theater.' We had a ritual of watching it on Sundays."

"I really miss 'Wild Wild West.' "

Peer relations

"I asked my friend Clark to come and sleep over and he said, 'What are we going to do at *your* house, sit around and listen to the radio?' "

"I'm ashamed to ask anybody over. It just feels weird because all the other kids have TV."

Punishment

"No TV was always our most effective threat. Of course we couldn't use it during the experiment."

What effect did a period without television have on the subsequent viewing habits of the families involved in the experiment? In follow-up interviews it was learned that in spite of the favorable changes noted during the no-television period by all the families taking part in the experiment, none of them chose to *continue* living without television. However, the parents seemed to look back on the no-television period with a certain amount of nostalgia, and to regard their return to television viewing with some regret:

"All four kids were fighting over what to watch. My husband and I looked at each other and realized how nice the summer had been without TV—we had forgotten about all those fights that centered around the television set."

"Turning off the TV for the summer was relatively simple. The kids just accepted the fact with the few exceptions noted in the diary. Our problems began when we turned it back on. Our eight-year-old (the family addict) went back to sneaking programs at times he wasn't supposed to watch. The kids went back to watching cartoons in the morning before school, and that took care of those nice family breakfasts we had all enjoyed."

"When we resumed watching, the kids didn't seem nearly as interested in TV—but they are getting into the old pattern as time goes on. And I know I am! That's why I think it's a good idea to do this once in a while."

"When the TV blackout was over, I tried limiting the kids' viewing to two hours a day, but as time goes on, I find them turning on the TV when they get up and only turning it off at bedtime. It's not that they're particularly interested in TV, but they're bored with the season and biding time until school opens again."

Some of the children themselves expressed a certain ambivalence about their resumption of a heavy viewing schedule.

"It's really harder to do other things when the TV is around. I just want to watch it."

"During the experiment I got my mind off TV so I

didn't keep thinking about it. Then I had more fun. I had to kick the habit."

Why Did They Go Back?

In light of the reported improvements in children's behavior and family life during these three experiments, why did these families resume their old patterns of television viewing instead of perpetuating the notable improvements by getting rid of television permanently?

"Did you ever consider living without television for good?" Brawley was asked.

"No," he answered after a few moments of thought, "I really never even considered that. You'd wonder why, wouldn't you? It reminds me of the time I was sick, a while back, and had to give up smoking. I said, 'Oh, I feel so much better because I'm not smoking. I've got my wind back and I feel great!' But as soon as the doctor said I was all right again, I went right back to cigarettes. Well, I suppose TV's a habit, too. You enjoy it, but when you think about it, television doesn't offer much that you couldn't replace by yourself, or do a lot better. But still, once you've got the habit, it's hard to do without it. Like cigarettes."

A psychologist asked to give an opinion as to why the no-television experiments did not lead families to give up television suggests that the parents were in fact deceiving themselves, that while they thought they *ought* to engage in the activities they took up during the no-television period—reading, playing games, conversing—these didn't fulfill the needs that television viewing did. That, he suggests, is why they went back to television.

But what *are* the needs that television fulfills? The need for passivity, for self-annihilation, for regression to a state of dependence . . . surely habitual television viewing serves few needs more auspicious than these. Perhaps a life of activity, of self-searching and growth, seems too difficult to attempt in our fragmented modern society. And yet the tone of ruefulness with which parents described their return to a television-dominated family life suggests one of the oldest conflicts of human nature. In the Bible Paul puts it in these words: "For what I would, that do I not; but what I hate, that do I."

17

Giving Up Television for Good

Yet some families *do* choose to live without television for good. Of these, some begin family life without a television set and bring up their children without one. Others (although there are no statistics, a casual survey indicates that their number is far greater) give up television after a period of time during which they owned a set and watched regularly.

Often the decision to get rid of the set for good is precipitated by an involuntary period of no television —the set breaks, the roof aerial blows down during a storm. Sometimes the decision follows a long trip during which television was unavailable. It is during such televisionless periods that parents seem to gain perspective on their television problem and come to the realization that something can be done about it:

"The set was controlling our lives," a Denver father reports. "We argued with the kids about what they should watch. The kids argued with each other about what to watch. The kids didn't want to come to dinner because they were watching something. The biggest arguments we had in the family were over the damn TV set. When it broke down one day, we came to our senses. Let's see what happens, we said, and we never had another set after that."

Like the no-television experiment families, those who have given up television for good are valuable sources of information about the changes that occur when television is eliminated. But while the experiment families soon returned to the "before" condition in the before-after conjunction, those who gave up television for good had the strength, for as yet undetermined reasons, to hang on to the "after." The following brief histories describe four such families.

1. Too Hard to Control

The Gerbers are a family who found television too hard to control and decided to do without it. Jim and Barbara Gerber live in a large apartment in New York. Jim is a writer and Barbara is a graduate student in sociology. Their children, Ned and Annie, are now 15 and 13 years old. Barbara describes their family struggles with the television problem and their solution: no television at all. At the time of the interview (without Jim Gerber, who was out of town), the Gerbers had been without television for almost a year.

"When we had the television it was always the source of complaints and terrible fights. We kept trying out new systems to deal with it. Each system would break down and then we'd fight about the system itself. The whole thing was terrible. The government, the regulation, of television was consuming an enormous amount of time and energy.

"At first we had no rules. But it turned out that Ned would watch all day if he could. And then the kids would argue about what programs to watch, who would have first choice. We couldn't afford to get another set. And even if we *had* gotten another set, we would have wanted a color TV and that would have opened up a new area of potential fighting about who would get to watch the color set.

"But besides the squabbling, television caused other problems. For one thing family dinner used to be arranged around television programs. Either somebody said, 'I can't eat until eight o'clock because I'm watching "Mission Impossible," ' or 'I've got five minutes to eat dinner because "Mission Impossible" is coming on.' So dinner always turned out to be something sandwiched in between two programs.

"And when the kids had friends come over, they were very likely to watch television together instead of playing. I'd come in and find them all in the zombie position, huddled around the television set. That would bother me and I'd turn it off and tell them to play. But do you know something extraordinary? Sometimes they'd sit there and stare at the set for minutes after I'd turn it off!

"It just amazes me to think that we could have lived in this horrible style for so many years. Why didn't we get rid of the television set long ago? I sometimes wonder. But actually I know the answer to that question. I really and truly needed television when the kids were little.

"I was stuck with two small kids, a year and a half apart, in a New York apartment, with no help of any kind. There was no backyard. There was no kind of activity around except what I could dream up for them to do around the house. And so I used the television set a lot. I don't think I would have survived without it.

"In those days I let the kids watch as much television as they wanted, mostly because I wanted them to watch just as much as they did. But it turned out that Ned watched a lot more than Annie. He'd sit for hours in front of the set, sucking his thumb. He'd go into a real trance when he watched TV. Sometimes he'd watch for six, seven hours. He never got tired of watching television.

"Of course, I felt terribly guilty about it. I didn't think all that TV was good. But I rationalized. I was exhausted. I needed it. My husband was working day and night making ends meet in those days, so he couldn't help me.

"A year ago we came back from a summer out in the West, two months completely away from television. And we just decided we'd had it. We unplugged the set and put it away in a closet. And it's been there ever since, except for the World Series and special things like that, when we go to all the trouble of bringing it out again."

An interviewer asked Barbara Gerber, Ned, and Annie how they felt about life without a television set in their house.

"I *love* not having television," the mother answered, "even though I used to enjoy watching quite a bit. I feel as if I've been handed a gift of a few extra hours every day. Not just the time I myself spent watching, but all the time I spent adjudicating fights about it and dealing with it. I love not having to feel resentful that I have something to do instead of being able to watch some program I wanted to see. I love not having to read *TV Guide*, not having to *look* for *TV Guide*. I love not being mad that I missed a program I could have watched last night. I don't feel sorry about not having TV, not one little bit."

What about Ned, the most avid watcher in the family? His mother reported being surprised that Ned had not complained about the decision to eliminate television. Ned described his feelings about it:

"I think it's a lot better now. See, what Annie does is she'll do her homework right away when she gets home from school and get it all over with. Not me. I'd always wait until the last minute. It was always such a temptation when the TV was around—I'd just keep putting off my work. I always felt guilty. I knew I should be doing my work. But I'd watch TV anyhow.

"Now I usually end up reading one of my books for school, especially science, which I really like. Before, when we had TV I'd never read a book. Never. If I had reading to do for a course, I'd put it off and figure I'd just listen to the discussion in class and take it from there. But now with no TV, I'm sort of *forced* to read. There's nothing else to do."

Annie was not as emphatic, but did not disagree:

"Yes, I guess we're better off without television. We talk more at dinner. Everybody tells what they did all day, and all that. But I never watched as much TV as Ned, so it doesn't make so much difference to me whether we have it or not. And I do miss some programs. And also it's hard sometimes because teachers sometimes assign things to watch on TV. But I'm pretty satisfied with our life without television."

The Gerbers presented a fine picture of family harmony and contentment. Did all those years of television viewing have no damaging effects? For if they did not, why not use television without limit when children are young and troublesome, as Barbara Gerber did, and then get rid of it when the going is easier? A final comment by Ned left the question in the air:

"The way it used to be I didn't care what program I watched as long as I was watching *something*. It could have been 'Popeye' or 'Sesame Street' or the United Nations, anything. But now I spend more time out of the house. I *do* read more when I'm home, but mostly I try to stay out of the house as long as possible. Because I have a feeling that I have nothing to do at home now. I'm just not used to figuring out things to do. See, when we had the TV, I didn't notice I was doing nothing when I watched all those hours. But now I notice."

2. *It Takes Time to Get Television Out of Your System*

The four Davis kids live with their parents in a large farmhouse surrounded by woods and fields in northern New York State. They are aged 4, 7, 10, and 13 years. On a warm spring day two years ago instead of romping outdoors, instead of picking flowers growing wild around the house or climbing the fruit trees nearby, instead of peering into the woodchuck hole or watching the fish swim in the clear stream behind their house, the four children sat in a row on the long sofa in the living room and stared ahead of them at a small table where a short time ago the television set had stood. It was gone.

"They really sat there for quite a while, just as if they were watching," their mother reported. "It was pathetic. But it made us absolutely certain that we'd done the right thing by chucking the set out."

The aerial on the roof had blown down and broken in a storm, and without it there was no television reception.

"It would have cost an arm and a leg to buy a new one and get it installed. Besides we were fed up with all the television watching we were doing—the kids and us, too. We were pretty addicted. The set was on most of the time. So we decided to get rid of the set and see what happened," said Mrs. Davis.

"The first few weeks without the set were hard. The kids wandered around like lost souls. They stayed indoors a lot and got in my hair. I'd send them out and they didn't know what to do with themselves.

"Saturday mornings was when I missed the set the most. That was when we used to stay in bed a nice long time while the kids sat in the living room, glued to the set, quiet, not moving hardly. Now they were after us for this and that, or they'd be fighting or getting into some kind of trouble.

"But gradually things got better. They began playing games with each other, something they'd never gone in for much, even though we *had* all the games—Chinese checkers, Monopoly, Parcheesi.

"They sort of had to learn to play with each other, and after a while they began to fight a lot less.

"Then they began to spend more and more time outdoors. This happened gradually. The oldest boy began fishing a lot. And he and his younger brother got interested in the woodchuck and spent lots of time waiting for him to come out of his hole. They'd never been interested in *anything* like that before. They asked for one of those traps that catches live animals and got one for Christmas. And after that they hardly set foot in the house before dark.

"This happened two years ago, and really, I think they're different kids now," said Mrs. Davis with a certain amount of surprise. "They even think so themselves. And they know our getting rid of the television has something to do with it. Nowadays, when they come back from a visit at a friend's house they feel critical. They'll talk about how much TV their friends watch, and how they don't do many interesting things.

"The funniest thing of all is that here we are all living in the country, and the kids are just beginning to be country kids. They talk about their friends as 'indoor kids,' can you imagine? But it took time. You can't just turn off your set for a few days and expect anything to change much. It takes time to get television out of your system."

3. "Like Old-Fashioned Living"

In July 1972 Paul and Bea Warner and their boys closed up their house on the outskirts of Pittsburgh, left their dogs at a neighbor's, and went to Africa for six months. Adam was 11, Peter 9. It was Paul's sabbatical from his university's music department, and with the help of a small grant he intended to spend the time away from his teaching duties writing music. He needed a change of scene, he felt; his best works had been written far from home.

"Before we left for Africa," Bea said, "the boys were really addicted to television. The 'Three Stooges' after school, endless cartoons. I'd be in the kitchen cooking and I could hear the dialogue from the set. Without ever seeing the show, I could tell it was the fifteenth time they'd watched the same damn program. It made me furious. I'd yell at them to go outside and I don't think they ever heard me—they'd be in a stupor.

"We tried to get them not to watch so much. We were always laying down all sorts of rules and regulations: you can't watch until you finished practicing or until your homework is done or whatever. It was a real struggle. The way they'd practice when they were rushing to see some program was probably worse than not practicing at all. It really upset us, especially Paul. Because both kids really wanted to play an instrument. It wasn't as if we were pushing them. But you've got to practice if you want to learn an instrument and practicing is hard. If there's something easier to do, like watch TV, what kid is going to want to practice?"

When the Warners arrived in Africa, they stayed, as prearranged, in the comfortable house of another academic American family who had returned to America for a year. The house was filled with books and games. But there was no television set. Television had simply not come to that area.

"Of course, we *were* in a foreign country, a pretty exotic one at that," said Bea, "and there was a lot for the boys to see and take in. It wasn't as if we had gone cold turkey from television back home. But still, six months is a long time and we were all thrown on our own resources quite a lot. The first thing we noticed was that the kids began to do a lot more reading than they had ever done at home. I guess it was out of sheer boredom. Peter had always been a good reader, but Adam had never liked to read much. Now he started reading like a house on fire. He read all the nature books around and got really interested in the wild life around us. There was a junior encyclopedia in the house, and they started with 'A' and began to plough through it! It was really amazing. Paul and I couldn't believe it.

"But the biggest difference was that we began to do a lot of talking together. It was like old-fashioned living, somehow. The four of us sat around and just talked about everything. We talked and talked. We talked about socialism because we were in a socialist country. We talked about racial problems. We talked about music, about books.

"Actually, the timing was perfect. The kids were old enough to talk to, but still young enough to be dependent on us. And so they had to adhere to our routine, in a way. And they couldn't just go off somewhere and do their own thing, like watch television, because they had no special thing of their own there. We had to find *common* things, if you see what I mean. I'll never forget those months.

"When we came home we decided that there was no reason why we shouldn't keep on talking together, why the boys shouldn't keep on reading a lot of books. We made up our minds to get rid of our set.

"It's not the same as in Africa, of course. The kids across the street have television, and so on. But things are better. The kids still read more. They seem to have a lot more time on their hands. They do hang around the house a lot, it seems, and sometimes they drive me crazy. But sometimes, just out of nowhere, they'll start to do something interesting, like make up a cross-word puzzle, or start a collection. And they do a lot more practicing nowadays, pretty much voluntarily."

4. Ousting the Stranger from the House

Colman McCarthy, a *Newsweek* columnist, describes the results of eliminating television:

When I turned off the television for the last time about a year ago and dumped the set for good, some friends, relatives and unasked advisers on the block predicted I would not last long without it. Few disputed the common gripe that TV is a wasteland, with irrigation offered only by the rare trickle of a quality program. Instead, they doubted that the addiction of some twenty years before the tube could be stilled by this sudden break with the past. It is true that an addiction had me, my veins eased only by a fix of 30 to 35 hours a week; my wife's dosage was similar, and our children—three boys under 7—already listened more to the television than to us.

Now, a year later—a family living as cultural cave men, says an anthropologist friend—the decision we made was one of the wisest of our married life. The ratings—our private Nielsens—during this year of setlessness have been high, suggesting that such common acts as talking with one's children, sharing ideas with one's wife, walking to the neighborhood library on a Saturday morning, quiet evenings of reading books and magazines aloud to each other, or eating supper as a family offer more intellectual stimulation than anything on television.

The severity of an addiction to TV is not that it reduces the victim to passivity while watching it but that it demands he be a compulsive activist to get in front of it. If I arrived home at 6, for example, and dinner was ready at 6:25—my wife's afternoon movie had run late—I would shove down the food in five minutes. The deadline, falling like a guillotine, was at 6:30. Chancellor came on then, Cronkite at 7; if CBS was dull, Smith and Reasoner were on ABC. If I hadn't finished dinner, I would sprint back to the table during the commercials for short-order gulps, then back to cool John, Uncle Walter or wry Harry. My wife, desperate Mav, was left at the table to control the bedlam of the kids, caused by my in-and-out sprints. The chaos I heard coming from the dining room was fitting: it was matched by the chaos in the world reported on the evening news, except the latter, in the vague "out there," was easier to handle.

With the set gone, these compulsions and in-turnings have gone too. We eat dinner in leisure and peace now. We stay at the playground until the children have had enough fun, not when I need to rush home to watch the 4 p.m. golf. Occasionally, my wife and I have the exotic experience of spending an evening in relaxed conversation, not the little half-steps of talk we once made in a forced march to Marital Communication. In those days, we would turn off the set in midevening and be immediately oppressed by the silence.

What had been happening all those years of watching television, I see now, was not only an addiction but also, on a deeper level, an adjustment. All of us had become adjusted to living with a stranger in the house. Is there any more basic definition of a television set than that?[1]

18

No Television Ever

The number of families in America who choose to live without television is small indeed, since at least 95.5 percent of all occupied households have at least one television set. A small number of these no-television families have never owned a television set.

Among them are those who have decided to live without television because they simply do not like it. "We didn't want TV because we felt we had no time for it," and "As newlyweds we saw no real need for a TV, and after periodic reconsiderations we still feel the same—TV just isn't important to us," are among the reasons given for the decision to eschew television completely.

Some couples avoid acquiring a television when they first set up housekeeping out of fear that they will not be able to control it. "I was worried that I might watch too much. That's what used to happen when I lived at home. I'd sit in front of that thing all day," explains a Denver father. "Why bring the enemy into the house?" says a New Mexico father to explain the absence of a television set in his home.[1]

The parents and children of families who have never had television in their homes present a solid front: among the thirteen no-television-ever families interviewed for this book, not a single parent or child expressed the desire to acquire a television set.

Indeed a feeling of pride that sometimes borders on the self-satisfied often characterizes the no-television-ever family. "We don't have a TV because our family does other things and has more fun," says an eight-year-old. "A lot of the kids I know watch TV all the time—it's pathetic," says a ten-year-old. "The kids take pride that we don't have a TV," a mother reports. "They like to be able to say that we don't have TV." This contrasts sharply with the situation that often exists among families who give up television after years of viewing. In these families resentment about the elimination of television may run high among the children, at least for a time.

No-television parents are often asked if they find the job of bringing up children much harder in the absence of a television set. But these parents often believe their life is easier, partly because their children are more resourceful, and partly because an area of conflict has been eliminated.

"I object to people who think that I must have a lot of patience to manage my kids without TV," states a Denver mother. "I *don't* have a lot of patience at all. But the kids have plenty of things that keep them occupied. I never hear them say, 'What shall I do now?' "

"There *is* that hour or so when you're trying to prepare dinner when it might be nice to send the kids off to watch TV," allows a New York mother of three children. "That's the time of day they're most obnoxious. They're hungry and tired, and I'm hungry and tired, too. But a little bit of healthy mayhem and yelling and screaming at each other works up our appetite, I guess. By dinnertime everything is all right. It's a small price to pay for all the advantages of life without television."

"The only disadvantage no-television families mention is the difficulty of attracting baby-sitters to a televisionless home:

"My biggest problem is baby-sitters. If you don't have a television, they come with great reluctance. I try to lure them by telling them about the stereo and allowing them to make all the phone calls they want, but it's a big problem," notes one no-television-ever mother with two small children, adding, "If anything would cause us to get a set, it would be to make it easier to get baby-sitters."

The no-television-ever families are characterized by more family conversation, much of it occurring during meals. They seem to spend considerably more time eating together than other families.

"We have house guests who are always surprised when they come down to breakfast and find us all there talking together. Sometimes we sit at the breakfast table for an hour and a half. But we all go to bed terribly early, shockingly early, and get up early as well," relates one mother.

Other no-television-ever families report a similar tendency to linger at mealtimes, more frequently dinner than breakfast, however. That this is related to their lack of television is suggested by the reports of former television-owning families, who frequently mention longer and more chatty meals after television has been eliminated. Early bedtimes are also commonly mentioned by no-television-ever families, as well as by those who have given up television.

When families give up television they often try to replace viewing time with games and family activities. But no-television-ever families give little evidence of playing more with their children than other parents. "We don't really play games at all, as a family," says a mother of two school-age children. "To tell the truth, I don't like to play games. But we do an awful lot of talking together."

How, then, *do* these families spend their free time, especially those evening hours that other families spend watching television?

"Reading by ourselves, each separately," answers one mother. "And in the summertime the boys will stay outside playing until bedtime."

Practicing a musical instrument takes up children's time in many of these households. Pianos were playing in four out of ten no-television households surveyed by *The New York Times* in an article about no-television families.[2]

Some of the time families might have spent watching television is spent listening to the radio and to records, activities that are considered "functionally similar" to television viewing (the three are often lumped together in a single category by researchers). A number of no-television-ever parents report that they and their children spend time listening to records of stories and plays and the like, not merely musical records. But these parents do not refer to their children's involvement with fantasy on records in a critical or anxious way, as many parents do to their children's television involvement. "You use your imagination in listening to records or stories on the radio," one mother noted. Another parent observed that "sometimes my five-year-old is tired and uses a record to relax, but she often falls asleep before the record is over. I don't think kids who zonk out with television actually fall asleep while watching. They just sit there in a daze."

Unlike families who give up television after years of viewing and often feel evangelistic about their new way of life, no-television-ever families tend to be reticent about their televisionless status:

"We seldom mention it to people, although neighbors discover our TV-less home from their children," says one father.

"We just don't talk about TV with our friends. Most people don't even know we don't have a set, except for our closer friends. They'll ask if we saw such-and-such program and we'll say no, we missed it, without going into our not having a TV," reports a mother.

Perhaps the reticence of no-television-ever families is an acquired defense against the prickly reactions of many parents when confronted with an anti-television argument, especially when voiced in the somewhat self-righteous tone that characterizes converts to a cause.

"We have been accused many times of culturally depriving our children" says one mother who does not hesitate to air her low opinion of television and her delight in her family life without it. "You'd be amazed at how emotional and angry people can become when you express the idea that you don't approve of television. It's worse than attacking motherhood or apple pie. We take our four children to concerts and museums and don't feel they're deprived of culture. On the contrary, I'm well pleased with their physical, mental, and emotional development—they're active, eager, curious, independent *doers*. They love to read, do well in school, and have good imaginations. They never run out of things to do."

Though sometimes guilty of smugness, no-television-ever families may well have something to be smug about. As one such parent reports:

"People always ask me accusingly, 'Don't you want your children to watch "Sesame Street?"' But we're a very close family and we don't want any built-in separaters cutting us off from each other. We read a lot, talk a lot, listen to music. Once in a while we'll rent a set for a special occasion like the Watergate hearings or a big sports event. But for us television is like junk food—a once-in-a-while thing."

Afterword

There are two ways to consider television in our society. Its use and overuse may be seen as symptoms of other modern ills: alienation, dehumanization, apathy, moral vacuum. Or one can regard the television set as a pathogen, a *source* of such symptoms. The tone of helplessness that surrounds the issue of television—"it's here and it's part of our lives, and there's nothing we can do about it"—reveals the prevalence of the first way of thinking.

It would be foolish to deny that there are many serious, perhaps even incurable afflictions that beset us in a society increasingly dominated by technology. There are many aspects of modern life that are indeed beyond our control. Frightening inroads have been made into the formerly inviolable privacy of our homes and families both by the lawful activities of the government and by the illegal invasions of antisocial forces whose number seems to be ever growing. We feel increasingly helpless, and our dependence on television is surely a reflection of this helplessness. For if activity is futile in modern society, if our efforts are meaningless in the face of an uncontrollable and unfathomable bureaucracy, then why not settle into the pleasures of total passivity?

This attitude lies behind the common rationalizations that are heard regarding the role of television in children's lives.

A television executive says: "There are many families where the child who watches television wouldn't be getting anything better from the parents. The more indifferent the parents you are dealing with, the more useful a tool television becomes."

This way of thinking is a good example of what has been called "Robinsonism"[1]—a tendency to apply a hypothesis of total isolation (such as on Robinson Crusoe's island) to a situation in which isolation does not actually exist. It is Robinsonism to say "better a good photograph than a bad portrait" or "better an attractive hallucination than an ugly reality," since each statement presupposes the necessity of choosing between only two alternatives, when, in fact, other alternatives *are* available.

The argument that television abuse is acceptable because it replaces an even more unattractive way of life is fallacious because it implies that a better way of life does not exist. But other alternatives *do* exist for a child in an unfortunate family situation, for instance, or a child with indifferent parents. The presence of television in the home, however, and the child's dependence on it for those gratifications that should come from his family relationships, can only increase his parents' indifference and perpetuate the pathological situation.

Dorothy Cohen, professor of education and perhaps the single influential professional who has spoken unequivocally about the destructive role of television in children's lives, observes:

"The impact of television on so-called disadvantaged children has been minimal in terms of goals such as learning to read—but its impact on their development has been great. It has robbed them of their normal opportunities to talk, to play, to *do*. It has interfered with their normal opportunities to grow. The big thing for me is the protection of children during the period of vulnerability in their lives. I think children under five should not watch television at all. But nobody is going to pay much attention to that. I say that kind of thing strongly and dramatically so at least people will come back with a slightly better compromise. Ideally I think young children should not watch television, but I'm afraid that's really an impossible thing to accomplish."[2]

But an awareness of television's potentially pathogenic influence on young children's ways of thinking and behaving may lead parents to reconsider their acceptance of television as an inevitable part of their children's lives. It may change their focus from *what* their children are watching to why and how much they are watching, and what they are missing as a result. An understanding of the changes in child rearing brought about by the availability of television as a sedative for active and troublesome preschoolers, changes that lead to poorer socialization of children, may cause parents to decide that their difficulties as parents are ultimately increased, not alleviated, as a result of their use of television as a source of relief. And finally, a consideration of the inroads television makes into family life, its effects on meals, conversations, games, rituals, may persuade parents that the price of accepting television as a force in the family is too high to pay.

For although we may be powerless in the face of the abstract machine that modern society has become, we can still assert our wills in the face of that real and tangible machine in our homes, the television set. We can learn to control it so that it does not control us.

Notes

PREFACE

1. Philip Slater, *The Pursuit of Loneliness* (Boston: Beacon Press, 1972).

1. IT'S NOT WHAT YOU WATCH

1. *Nielsen Television Index, Report on Television Usage* (A. C. Nielsen Co., Hackensack, N.J.).
2. Leonard LoSciuto, "A National Inventory of Television Viewing Behavior," *Television and Social Behavior: A Technical Report to the Surgeon General's Scientific Advisory Committee on Television and Social Behavior*, Vol. IV (Washington D.C.: United States Government Printing Office, 1971).
3. Aletha H. Stein and Lynette K. Friedrich, "Television Content and Young Children's Behavior," *Television and Social Behavior*, Vol. II.
4. Benjamin Spock, *Baby and Child Care* (New York: Pocket Books, 1963).
5. *Ibid*, 1968 edition.
6. Evelyn Kaye Sarson, "How TV Threatens Your Child," *Parents' Magazine*, August, 1972.
7. Quoted in Norman Morris, *Television's Child* (Boston: Little, Brown, 1971).
8. Sedulus, "Sesame Street," *New Republic*, June 6, 1970.
9. Nathan Talbot, *Raising Children in Modern America* (Boston: Little, Brown, 1976).
10. Nat Rutstein, *Go Watch TV!* (New York: Sheed and Ward, 1974).
11. Joyce Maynard, "Growing Up with TV," *TV Guide*, July 5, 1975.
12. Jack Gould, "Family Life 1948 AT (After Television)," *The New York Times*, August 1, 1948.

2. A CHANGED STATE OF CONSCIOUSNESS

1. Quote from personal interview, May 7, 1975.
2. T. Berry Brazleton, "How to Tame the TV Monster," *Redbook*, April, 1972.
3. Letter from Matthew Dumont, M.D., *American Journal of Psychiatry*, Vol. 133, April, 1976.
4. Dr. Werner I. Halpern, quoted in Philip Jones, "The Educational TV in Your School May Be Anything But Educational," *The American School Board Journal*, March, 1974.

5. Gerald Lesser, *Children and Television* (New York: Random House, 1974).

3. TELEVISION ADDICTION

1. Lawrence Kubie, *Neurotic Distortion and the Creative Process* (Lawrence: University of Kansas Press, 1958).
2. Stanton Peele and Archie Brodsky, *Love and Addiction* (New York: Taplinger, 1975).
3. Les Brown, "Democrats Reach Low TV Audience," *The New York Times*, January 25, 1975.
4. Cyclops, "The West Coast—Is It Live or on Tape?" *The New York Times*, July 20, 1975.
5. John Cheever, *Bullet Park* (New York: Alfred A. Knopf, 1967).

4. VERBAL AND NONVERBAL THOUGHT

1. S. Ball and G. Bogatz, *The First Year of Sesame Street: An Evaluation*, and *The Second Year of Sesame Street: A Continuing Evaluation* (Princeton, N.J.: Educational Testing Service, 1970, 1971).
2. Thomas D. Cook, Hilary Appleton, Ross F. Conner, Ann Shaffer, Gary Tamkin, and Stephen J. Weber, *"Sesame Street" Revisited* (New York: Russell Sage Foundation, 1975).
3. Bernard Z. Friedlander, Harriet S. Wetstone, Christopher S. Scott, "Suburban Preschool Children's Comprehension of an Age-Appropriate Informational Television Program," *Child Development*, Vol. 45, 1974.
4. Leifer, Collins, Gross, Taylor, Andrews, and Blackmer, "Developmental Aspects of Variables Relevant to Observational Learning," *Child Development*, 1970.
5. Coates and Hartup, "Age and Verbalization in Observational Learning," *Developmental Psychology*, Vol. 1, 1969.
6. See Eric H. Lenneberg, "On Explaining Language," *Science*, May 9, 1969, for a discussion of brain lateralization.
7. The idea of two disparate forms of mental organization was suggested by Arthur J. Deikman, "Bimodal Consciousness," *Archives of General Psychiatry*, December, 1971.
8. Ralph N. Haber, "Eidetic Images," *Scientific American*, April, 1969.
9. Jerome Kagan, *Change and Continuity in Infancy* (New York: John Wiley & Sons Inc., 1971).
10. Ned O'Gorman, "The Children," *The New York Times Magazine*, June 1, 1975.
11. Mark R. Rosenzweig, Edward L. Bennet, and Marian Cleeves Diamond, "Brain Changes in Response to Environment," *Scientific American*, February, 1972.
12. Among these studies are: H. Skeels, "Adult Status of Children with Contrasting Early Life Experiences," *Monographs on Social Research in Child Development*, Vol. 31, 1966; Coleman and Provence, "Environmental Retardation in Infants Living in Families," *Pediatrics*, Vol. 19, 1957; R. Spitz, "Hospitalism," *Psychoanalytic Study of the Child*, Vol. 1, 1945; W. Goldfarb, "Ef-

fects of Psychological Deprivation in Infancy and Subsequent Stimulation," *American Journal of Psychiatry*, Vol. 102, 1945.

13. Wiesel and Hubel, "Effects of Visual Deprivation on Morphology and Physiology of Cells in Cats' Lateral Geniculate Body," *Journal of Neurophysiology*, Vol. 26, 1963.

14. A. Riesen, "Arrested Vision," *The Nature and Nurture of Behavior*, ed. Greenough (San Francisco: W. H. Freeman Co., 1973).

15. See Maya Pines, "Head Head Start," *The New York Times Magazine*, October 26, 1975, and Urie Bronfenbrenner, "Is Early Intervention Effective?" report for Department of Health, Education, and Welfare (Washington, D.C., 1974).

16. See Christopher Jencks, *Inequality* (New York: Basic Books, 1972).

17. Quoted in Lucien Malson, *Wolf Children and the Problem of Human Nature* (New York: Atlantic Monthly Press, 1972).

5. TELEVISION AND READING

1. A discussion of the "acoustic" image of words is found in H. J. Chaytor's *From Script to Print* (London: W. Heffer and Sons, 1950).

2. Bruno Bettelheim, "Parents vs. Television," *Redbook*, November 1963.

3. Tony Schwartz, *The Responsive Chord* (New York: Anchor/Doubleday, 1973).

4. Much of the material in this section is based on a reading of Julian Hochberg and Virginia Brooks' "The Perception of Television Displays," a prepublication draft of a survey and analysis of the basic perceptual determinants that may affect viewers' responses to the television experience, commissioned by the Television Laboratory at WNET/13.

5. *Ibid.*

6. Quoted in Martin Mayer, *About Television* (New York: Harper and Row, 1972).

7. Lyle and Hoffman, "Explorations in Patterns of Television Viewing by Preschool-age Children," *Television and Social Behavior*, Vol. IV.

8. J. Feeley, "Interest and Media Preference of Middle Grade Children," *Reading World*, 1974.

9. George Steiner, "After the Book?" *Visual Language*, Vol. 6, 1972.

10. Quoted in Norman Morris, *Television's Child* (Boston: Little, Brown, 1971).

11. E. Parker, "The Effects of TV on Public Library Circulation," *Public Opinion Quarterly*, Vol. 127, 1963.

12. Andrew Malcolm, "Japan's Reading Craze at a Peak in Recession," *The New York Times*, March 26, 1976.

13. Gene Maeroff, "Rise in Remedial Work Taxing Colleges," *The New York Times*, March 7, 1976.

14. "Why Johnny Can't Write," *Newsweek*, December 8, 1975.

15. Quoted in *ibid.*

16. Quoted in *ibid.*

17. Jerzy Kosinski quoted in Horace Newcomb, *Television: The Critical View* (London: Oxford University Press, 1976).

6. TELEVISION AND VIOLENCE: A NEW APPROACH

1. "Skyrocketing Juvenile Crime," *The New York Times*, February 21, 1975.
2. Quoted from address to Child Study Association of America, 1961.
3. Edith Efron, "Does Television Violence Really Affect TV Viewers?" *TV Guide*, June 14, 1975.
4. Enid Nemy, "Violent Crime by Young People: No Easy Answers," *The New York Times*, March 17, 1975.
5. *Crime on Television: A Survey Report* (Los Angeles: National Association for Better Radio and Television, 1964).
6. *Nielsen Television Index* (A. C. Nielsen Co., Hackensack, N.J.).
7. Larry Gross, "The 'Real' World of Television," *Today's Education*, January-February, 1974.
8. Kurt Lang and Gladys Engel Lang, "The Unique Perspective of Television and Its Effects—A Pilot Study," *American Sociological Review*, February, 1953.
9. *Mainliner Magazine*, July, 1974.
10. See Roger Rosenblatt's "Residuals on an American Family," *New Republic*, November 23, 1974; for a discussion of the Loud family and their appearance on "An American Family."
11. See *The New York Times*, April 12, 1964, for an account of the Kitty Genovese murder.
12. Quoted by Edmund Carpenter in *Oh What a Blow That Phantom Gave Me* (New York: Holt, Rinehart, Winston, 1972).
13. Victor Cline, *The Desensitization of Children to Television Violence* (Bethesda, Md.: National Institute of Health, 1972).
14. Victor Cline, "Television Violence—How it Damages Your Children," *Ladies' Home Journal*, February, 1975.
15. Ted Morgan, "They Think 'I Can Kill Because I'm 14,'" *The New York Times Magazine*, January 19, 1975.
16. See "Youthful Violence Grows," *The New York Times*, November 4, 1974; and "Tale of a Young Mugger," *The New York Times*, April 11, 1976.
17. Quoted by Morgan, *op. cit.*
18. Quoted in "Youthful Violence Grows," *The New York Times*, November 4, 1974.
19. Dr. Denise Shine, head of the Rapid Intervention psychiatrists' office in Brooklyn Family Court, quoted in Morgan, *op. cit.*

7. TELEVISION AND PLAY

1. Lyle and Hoffman, "Explorations in Patterns of Television Viewing by Preschool-age Children," *Television and Social Behavior*, Vol. IV.
2. See Shramm, Lyle, Parker, *Television in the Lives of Our Children* (Stanford, Cal.: Stanford University Press, 1961) or Himmelweit, Oppenheim, Vince, *Television and the Child* (London:

Oxford University Press, 1958) for an investigation of this theory.

3. Lyle and Hoffman, *op. cit.*
4. Jerome Singer and Dorothy Singer, "A Member of the Family," *Yale Alumni Magazine,* March, 1975.
5. Stephen J. Suomi and Harry F. Harlow, "Monkeys at Play," *Natural History,* December, 1971.
6. Edward Norbeck, "Man at Play," *Natural History,* December, 1971.
7. "Many Rebels of the 1960's Depressed as They Near 30," *The New York Times,* February 29, 1976.

8. THE TELEVISION GENERATION

1. René Dubos, "The Despairing Optimist," *American Scholar,* Winter, 1975/76.
2. P. Whitty, "Studies of the Mass Media, 1949–1965," *Science Education,* 1966.
3. Lawrence Fuchs, *Family Matters* (New York: Random House, 1972).
4. Edward Fiske, "College Entry Tests Drop Sharply," *The New York Times,* September 7, 1975.
5. *Statistical Abstract of the U.S.* (Washington D.C.: Bureau of the Census, 1975).
6. *Nielson Television Index* (A. C. Nielsen Co., Hackensack, N.J.).
7. *Ibid.*
8. Lyle and Hoffman, "Explorations in Patterns of Television Viewing by Preschool-age Children," *Television and Social Behavior,* Vol. IV.
9. Shramm, Lyle, Parker, *op. cit.*
10. Lyle and Hoffman, *op. cit.*
11. Charles Reich, *The Greening of America* (New York: Random House, 1970).
12. Alvin Toffler, *Future Shock* (New York: Random House, 1970).
13. Theodore Roszak, *The Making of a Counter Culture* (New York: Doubleday, 1969).
14. Charles Reich, *op. cit.*
15. Theodore Roszak, *op. cit.*
16. *Uniform Crime Reports for the U.S.,* Federal Bureau of Investigation.
17. Norman E. Zinberg and John A. Robertson, *Drugs and the Public* (New York: Simon and Schuster, 1972).
18. Michael Shamberg, *Guerrilla Television* (New York: Holt, Rinehart, Winston, 1971).
19. Alvin Toffler, *op. cit.*
20. Quote from "The Effects of Marijuana on Consciousness," in Charles Tart, *Altered States of Consciousness* (New York: John Wiley and Sons, 1969).
21. *Ibid.*
22. Peter Martin and Allen Y. Cohen, *Understanding Drug Use* (New York: Harper and Row, 1971).
23. *Ibid.*

24. *Ibid.*
25. "Children of the Drug Age," *Saturday Review*, September 21, 1968.
26. Joyce Maynard, *Looking Back* (New York: Doubleday, 1972).

9. FAMILY LIFE

1. *The New York Times*, February 12, 1976.
2. Dorothy McFadden, "Television Comes to Our Children," *Parents' Magazine*, January, 1949.
3. Henrietta Battle, "TV and Your Child," *Parents' Magazine*, November, 1949.
4. Jack Gould, "What Is Television Doing to Us?" *The New York Times*, June 12, 1949.
5. Himmelweit, Oppenheim, Vince, *Television and the Child* (London: Oxford University Press, 1958).
6. Urie Bronfenbrenner, "Who Cares for America's Children?" Address presented at the Conference of the National Association for the Education of Young Children, 1970.
7. Eleanor Dienstag, "What Will the Kids Talk About? Proust?" *The New York Times*, December 24, 1972.
8. *Ibid.*
9. James H. Bossard and Eleanor S. Boll, *Ritual in Family Living* (Philadelphia: University of Pennsylvania Press, 1950).
10. Bossard and Boll, *The Sociology of Child Development* (New York: Harper and Row, 1960).
11. Ralph V. Extine, "Visual Interaction: The Glances of Power and Preference," in *Nonverbal Communication—Reading with Commentaries*, ed. Shirley Weitz (New York: Oxford University Press, 1974).
12. Bruno Bettelheim, *The Informed Heart* (New York: The Free Press, 1960).
13. Cyclops, "Watching the World Through TV-Colored Glasses," *The New York Times*, June 2, 1974.
14. E. Maccoby, "Television: Its Impact on School Children," *Public Opinion Quarterly*, Vol. 15, 1951.
15. R. Hamilton and R. Lawless, "Television within the Social Matrix," *Public Opinion Quarterly*, Vol. 20, 1956.
16. James Gabardino, "A Note on the Effects of Television Viewing," in Bronfenbrenner and Mahoney, *Influences on Human Development*, 2nd ed. (Hinsdale, Illinois: The Dryden Press, 1975).
17. Urie Bronfenbrenner, "The Origins of Alienation," *Scientific American*, August, 1974.
18. Irving Howe, "Notes on Mass Culture," *Politics*, Spring, 1948.
19. Jacques Ellul, *The Technological Society* (New York: Alfred A. Knopf, 1964).

10. PARENTS OF THE PAST

1. Lloyd de Mause, "The Evolution of Childhood," in *History of Childhood* (New York: Psychohistory Press, 1974).

2. *Ibid.*
3. From the "Diary of Cotton Mather," Vol. 1, quoted in *ibid.*

12. TELEVISION AND FREE TIME

1. Russell Hoban, *Nothing to Do* (New York: Harper and Row, 1964).
2. See John Bowlby, *Attachment and Loss* (New York: Basic Books, 1969).
3. See Selma Fraiberg, *The Magic Years* (New York: Charles Scribner's Sons, 1959).
4. J. Gewirtz, "A Factor Analysis of Some Attention-Seeking Behaviors of Young Children," *Child Development,* Vol. 27, 1956.
5. R. R. Sears, L. Rau, and R. Alpert, *Identification and Child Rearing* (Stanford, Cal.: Stanford University Press, 1965).

13. HOOKED PARENTS

1. Sharon Gadberry, "Television as Baby-sitter: A Field Comparison of Preschool Behavior During Playtime and During Television Viewing," *Child Development,* Vol. 45, 1974.

14. OUT OF CONTROL

1. *The New York Times Magazine,* February 2, 1975.
2. Nadine Brozan, "Film and TV Violence: A Nursery School Takes a Stand," *The New York Times,* June 1, 1975.
3. Robert Lewis Shayon, *Television and Our Children* (New York: Longman Green, 1951).
4. Lyle and Hoffman, "Explorations in Patterns of Television Viewing by Preschool-age Children," *Television and Social Behavior,* Vol. IV.
5. M. M. Haith, "The Response of the Human Newborn to Visual Movements," *Journal of Experimental Child Psychology,* Vol. 3, 1966.
6. Erich Fromm, *The Heart of Man* (New York: Harper and Row, 1964).
7. "Doctors Find TV Makes Child Ill," *The New York Times,* October 27, 1964.

15. CONTROLLING TELEVISION

1. Norman Morris, *Television's Child* (Boston: Little, Brown, 1971).
2. Nat Rutstein, *Go Watch TV!* (New York: Sheed and Ward, 1974).
3. Sarane Boocock, "Children and Society," paper prepared for the American Association for Advancement of Science, January, 1975.

16. BEFORE AND AFTER EXPERIMENTS

1. Used by permission of Don Brawley.
2. Barbara Haddad Ryan, "Would You Free Your Children from the Monster?" *Denver Post,* June 9, 1974.

17. GIVING UP TELEVISION FOR GOOD

1. Colman McCarthy, "Ousting the Stranger from the House," *Newsweek,* March 25, 1974.

18. NO TELEVISION EVER

1. New Mexico father quoted by Nadine Brozan, "No TV in the House and They Want It That Way," *The New York Times,* December 20, 1974.
2. *Ibid.*

AFTERWORD

1. Marshall McLuhan, *From Cliché to Archetype* (New York: Viking, 1970).
2. Dorothy Cohen, personal interview.

Index

ABOUT THE AUTHOR

MARIE WINN is the author of ten books for parents and children, including *The Playgroup Book, The Baby Reader* and *The Sick Book,* as well as articles for *The New York Times Magazine, The Village Voice* and other publications. Born in Czechoslovakia, she attended Radcliffe College and Columbia University, and now lives in New York with her husband, Allan Miller, and two young sons. The Millers own one small black-and-white television set that is used for special occasions.

Bantam Book Catalog

Here's your up-to-the-minute listing of over 1,400 titles by your favorite authors.

This illustrated, large format catalog gives a description of each title. For your convenience, it is divided into categories in fiction and non-fiction—gothics, science fiction, westerns, mysteries, cookbooks, mysticism and occult, biographies, history, family living, health, psychology, art.

So don't delay—take advantage of this special opportunity to increase your reading pleasure.

Just send us your name and address and 50¢ (to help defray postage and handling costs).